THE PEAK DISTRICT
& CENTRAL ENGLAND

EXPLORING WOODLAND

D1350476

WOODLAND
TRUST

THE PEAK DISTRICT & CENTRAL ENGLAND

Edited by Graham Blight

F

FRANCES LINCOLN LIMITED
PUBLISHERS

Acknowledgements

Introduction by Archie Miles
Site entries written by Sheila Ashton
Researched by Tim Hill & Diana Moss
Edited by Graham Blight
Maps by Linda M Dawes, Belvoir Cartographics & Design
Regional maps created using Maps in Minutes data © MAPS IN MINUTES™ 2004.
© Crown Copyright, Ordnance Survey 2004
Site maps © Woodland Trust

Photographic acknowledgements

Fran Hitchinson: 82
Karen Letten: 73
National Trust: 33, 45, 51,
Stuart Handley/Foto 45: 8, 27, 31, 35, 39, 46, 52, 75, 76, 85, 86, 89, 92, 94, 96, 100, 101, 105
Woodland Trust: 1, 2, 10 (Pete Holmes), 13, 15 (Roy Battell), 22 (Mike Brown), 25, 61, 65, 69, 71, 81, 87 (M Taylor), 90, 99

Frances Lincoln Ltd
4 Torriano Mews
Torriano Avenue
London NW5 2RZ
www.franceslincoln.com

The Peak District and central England
Copyright © Frances Lincoln 2006
Text © Woodland Trust 2006
Maps © see above

First Frances Lincoln edition: 2006

A catalogue record for this book is available from the British Library.

ISBN 10: 0-7112-2660-1
ISBN 13: 978-0-7112-2660-9

Printed and bound in Singapore
The paper used in this book was sourced from sustainable forests, managed according to FSC (Forest Stewardship Council) guidelines.

1 2 3 4 5 6 7 8 9

Half title page Ladybird, Battlestead Hill

Title page Blossom

Contents

How to use this guide

Covering a region that encompasses the Peak District and central England, this book is divided into four areas represented by key maps on pages 16–17, 36–37, 56–57 and 80–81. The tree symbols on these maps denote the location of each wood. In the pages following the key maps, the sites nearest one another are described together (wherever practical) to make planning a day out as rewarding as possible.

For each site entry the name of the nearest town/village is given, followed by road directions and the grid reference of the site entrance. The area of the site (in hectares followed by acres) is given together with the official status of the site where appropriate and the owner, body or organisation responsible for maintaining the site. Symbols are used to denote information about the site and its facilities as explained in the next column.

Type of wood

Mainly broadleaved woodland
Mainly coniferous woodland
Mixed woodland

Car park

Parking on site
Parking nearby
Parking difficult to find

Official status

Area of Outstanding Natural Beauty
AONB
Site of Special Scientific Interest SSSI

Site facilities

Sign at entry
Information board
One or more paths suitable for
  wheelchair users
Dogs allowed under supervision
Waymarked trail
Toilet
Picnic area
Entrance/car park charge
Refreshments on site

The Peak District & Central England

Sherwood Forest

Tread softly through the dappled shade of the forest. Keep your wits about you. Stop. Crouch down. Motionless beneath the bracken fronds sense the all-enfolding woodland life. Small birds chatter and squabble in the understorey and a jay shouts the odds through the canopy. A drowsy pollen-laden bumblebee blunders hopefully between the swaying foxgloves, and close by some unseen rodent rustles through the detritus of the forest floor seeking tasty morsels. There's nothing to be frightened of here, nothing to hide from, but the sunlight tirelessly plays tricks with the shadows. At first glance a bent, gnarled old forester, but an instant later the decrepit carcass of a venerable old oak glimpsed beyond the slender silver stems of young birches.

Robin Hood and his merry band may be merely distant memories of legend and hearsay, locked well away in the 12th or 13th century, but their medieval presence seems to be just out of sight in the next glade, particularly in Birklands; perhaps the finest remaining part of the vast sprawl of Sherwood Forest, which once covered 100,000 acres and stretched for some 25 miles north of Nottingham. Now part of the Sherwood Forest Country Park this is still one of the most extensive and atmospheric of ancient oak woods in the Midlands.

Some of the ancient oaks are up to 1,000 years old and, although many are decaying, they still possess a marvellous sculptural presence. They also provide outstanding habitats for all manner of bats, birds and insect life. In fact the area received its Site of Special Scientific Interest (SSSI) designation on the strength of its insects – more than 200 different spiders and almost 1,500 different beetles, some of which are unique to this site. The undoubted star of the forest is the Major Oak, now hollow and partly reliant on a network of props, hawsers and spars to hold it together. Estimated to be about 800–1,000 years old, it receives well over 800,000 visitors every year. A few years ago you could clamber all over this senior citizen of the forest, but visitor pressure was beginning to take its toll, so now you must view from a respectful distance.

Sherwood may be one of the highest profile woods in the Midlands, but the area has much else to offer. The general woodland type of oak with birch is one that proliferates throughout the central part of Nottinghamshire and also reaches to the eastern edges of Staffordshire, although it manifests in several different guises. At its finest the mature oaks, which will be prized by foresters for their timber, form the principal canopy with birch, the great coloniser, filling in the gaps caused by felling or natural decline. Coppice woods, cut on a 10–15 year rotation, contain a strong mix of oak, hazel and birch, with a scattering of rowan, field maple & holly. Some of these woods will have a few selected oaks which will be left as standards. On the poorest soils the oak and birch partnership is accompanied by Scots pine in an altogether more open woodland structure. Ash and field maple is the other most common type of woodland of the heavier clay soils of Nottinghamshire, whilst ash and wych elm tend to dominate the better-drained calcareous soils.

Hazelnuts

The soil types across the East Midlands vary a great deal, which is reflected by the dominant tree and plant species across the range. It is difficult to be categorical about the vegetation in any rigidly defined areas as there are a variety of bedrock incursions throughout. However there are a few distinctive woodland types linked to the geology of the region.

The Peak District of Derbyshire lies on carboniferous limestone; noted for its ash woods with associated wych elm and sycamore. Hazel is the most abundant shrub layer species, whilst hawthorn, rowan, field maple, whitebeam, dogwood, blackthorn, bird cherry and yew all feature strongly. By contrast there are tracts of gritstone here as well, Padley Gorge being a prime example of typical woodland, which supports oak and birch with some Scots pine and beech. The oak and birch mix also prevails on to the bunter sandstones found in Nottinghamshire. The Leicestershire woods are relatively sparse, with perhaps the most interesting sites to be found on the chalky boulder clays in the southeast, where woods tend to be composed mainly of an oak, ash and field maple mix, with shrubs such as elder, blackthorn, privet, and hawthorn forming the attendant understorey. On the eastern fringes of Leicestershire, and through into Lincolnshire, the prevailing Jurassic rocks manifest in calcareous blue clay or chalk, supporting woodlands of oak, ash, wych elm and in several sites considerable amounts of small-leaved lime; the latter being one of the principal species of the ancient wildwood.

Identifying rare species or site status indicators is all part of the fun of exploring woodland, and small-leaved lime is one tree that is a strong sign of ancient woodland. Pollen records reveal that this tree was once one of the pre-eminent species of lowland woods, but a combination of ancient woodland loss to agriculture, climatic changes which have seen a decline in its ability to set viable seed, and its susceptibility to intensive grazing has seen its decline. Where lime is found in woods it is most usually seen as coppice stools, and some of these can be of huge proportions indicating extremely great age. Those forming rings of stems 3–6 metres in diameter may be several thousand years old, making them potentially the oldest trees in Britain – even older than the most ancient churchyard yews!

It's important to realise that the woodland in evidence today is but a fragment of the almost continuous tree cover, often described as wildwood, which once stretched far and wide across Britain. From Neolithic times onwards people cleared trees in order to till the land and graze livestock; the cut timber provided fences to contain these animals, construction material for houses and a regular supply of firewood. Not all this led to the dramatic demise of woodland, for it didn't take the intellect of a genius to realise that without allowing some of the woodland to regenerate there would be a finite supply of timber and coppice wood. Moreover the fact was, and still is, that it's extremely difficult to obliterate broadleaf woodland simply by cutting it back. No sooner has a tree been cut than it begins to send out new shoots, a process harnessed in coppice and pollard management. Only the truly draconian measure of setting about trees with bulldozers will eradicate them completely and, sadly, this was often the fate of ancient woodland which was seen to be in the way of 'progress'. Unfortunately ancient woodland, Britain's rainforest, our richest habitat for wildlife, is still being lost to development today.

During the 18th and early 19th centuries many of the great landowners actually made major contributions to woodland regeneration, partly because they realised the potential revenue to be gleaned from commercial forestry, but also because they planted coverts to house their game and vast tracts of parkland to impress their neighbours and friends. The relentless tide of industrial progress on through the 19th century brought pressure to bear on woodland since vast quantities of coppice wood were required for charcoal and tan bark, but by the end of that century much had changed with the eclipsing of timber and charcoal as fuel in favour of coal and coke. This, coupled with the expansion of agriculture, began to change the hitherto relatively stable status of woodland.

Many of the larger broadleaf trees in today's woodland were planted in the mid-19th century with some purpose in mind, but with subsequent social and economic changes they were no longer needed. In many cases this has provided a legacy of handsome timber trees, but sometimes at the expense of coppice wood or understorey diversity.

The most ambitious woodland project to emerge in the Midlands in recent years has been the creation of the new National Forest, which aims to plant and maintain a great swathe of woodland from east Staffordshire through south Derbyshire and northwest Leicestershire where the landscape was previously dominated by the industrial sprawl of one of the country's largest coalfields. Now, working in close harmony with local landowners and the enthusiastic support of local communities, the seeds have been sown, or rather the saplings have been planted, of a whole new landscape and amenity for the future.

Take a walk in many a woodland which lies on accessible land and you'll almost certainly discover some degree of introduced conifers. Broadly speaking the most popular species have been Corsican pine, Norway spruce, Sitka spruce, Douglas fir, Western red cedar, and of course the native Scots pine, whilst oak, ash and beech have been popular hardwood choices. Even if your walk takes you through pure broadleaf woods it's quite likely that much of the tree cover will have been managed at some time, or will be the retained standards of an earlier generation of foresters. To find anything remotely approaching natural ancient woodland you must seek out those almost inaccessible locations, where man has always found it difficult to harvest timber, and his sheep and cattle have made few inroads with their relentless grazing. Here, natural regeneration creates vibrant woodland containing trees of various ages. Some of

Oak sapling

the best such examples are the steeper ash woods of the Derbyshire valleys, which have probably changed little over thousands of years. In some woods you'll find rivers or streams with the mosses, lichens and liverworts that such damp areas support, along with quaint little birds like dippers and wagtails bobbing from rock to rock. Water may exist in the form of ponds, either naturally occurring, or as the relict of some long-forgotten industry, and here it may be possible to find breeding colonies of frogs or newts whilst exotic-looking dragonflies patrol the surface. For the wettest of woodland sites look for the name 'car' or 'carr', (a name derived from the Anglo Saxon for such woods). Alder is usually the dominant species here, although there are also willow carrs. Tattershall Carrs in Lincolnshire is a splendid example although, in this case, a trifle drier than it might once have been due to extensive drainage systems to aid the surrounding agriculture.

Many woods with the best access contain wide rides which encourage butterflies and a greater variety of flowers. Carpets of wood anemones or bluebells are a glorious sight to behold in the spring, but the committed flower fanatic can find all manner of rarities in specific woods. You will rejoice the first time you come upon a scarce orchid or find a distinctive plant such as herb-paris or lily-of-the-valley; look to chalky soils for these specialities. With patience you can see a wonderful array of birdlife; after all, woods are the most diverse habitat for nesting birds. Find holes in trees for example, then wait and see what comes or goes. You might catch one of our three splendid woodpeckers or an owl. In the evenings watch for the emergence of several species of bats, or lie low to wait for badgers, foxes and deer to appear.

Woodland may harbour some remarkable treasures of nature, but it also conceals some surprising and fascinating historical evidence. The woods at Beacon Hill Country Park, in Leicestershire, surround what was once a Bronze Age settlement. Evidence of woodland protection in the shape of old boundary ditches and woodbanks often harks back to medieval times. No good having a productive coppice wood if your livestock invade it and graze off all the new growth! Holes in the ground usually relate to some kind of quarrying, often of considerable antiquity or, occasionally, old saw pits where foresters once cut their felled timber with mammoth two-man saws. Padley Woods, for example, contain evidence of quarrying for millstone grit – some of the old millstones still lie forgotten on the old quarry floor. Shallower depressions or, in some hillside woods, small platforms may indicate the past presence of charcoal hearths. Scrape a little surface loam away and discover the black evidence beneath.

So, when's the best time to head off into the woods? Well, any time; no matter what season there's always something different to see. Winter woodland on a chilly electric-blue day when hoar frost has picked out every last leaf and twig, or snow lies deep and crisp and even, casting a spell of muffled serenity. Early spring and golden

Frosted Holly

catkin-laden hazels glow like beacons as a stiff breeze propels you along the woodland path. Spring also turns the woodland floor into a mass of colour as flowers burst into bloom. Summer's myriad greens paint the canopy canvas and the heady scent of lime blossom fills the evening air, inducing slumbers. Or rustle and crunch into the pungent smell of autumn with its fireglow show.

Where you choose to go and what you want to see is down to you, and this book helps you make an informed decision. Most of the sites are managed to a greater or lesser degree, which means that rather than trying to dive into some tangled thicket you're assured of good access.

ARCHIE MILES

MAP 1

Longdendale Estate *p18*
Bitholmes Wood *p23*
Shire Hill *p18*
Wharncliffe Woods
Snake Woodlands *p20*
Tom Wood *p19*
Rivelin Valley
Bluebell Wood *p22*
Upper Derwent Woodlands *p21*
Ecclesall Wood
Padley Gorge *p26*
Burrs Wood *p*
Stand Wood

Peak District National Park

MAP 2 ▼(see p36)

10 miles

10 km

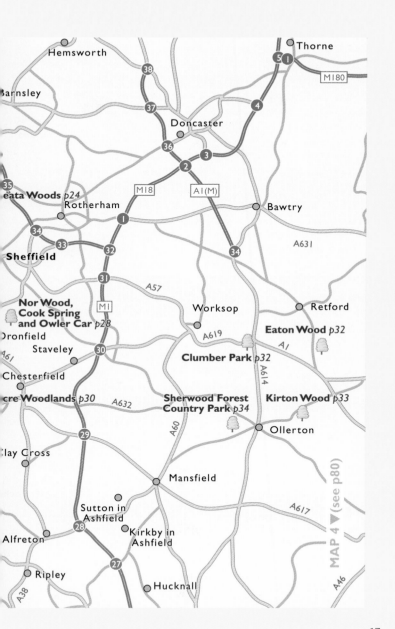

Hemsworth

Thorne

M180

Barnsley

38

37

Doncaster

4

36

2 3

M18 A1(M)

35

eata Woods p24
Rotherham

Bawtry

34

A631

1

33

32

34

Sheffield

31

A57

Retford

Nor Wood,
Cook Spring
and Owler Car p28

M1

Worksop

Eaton Wood p32

Dronfield

A619

Staveley

30

Clumber Park p32

A1

A614

A61

Chesterfield

cre Woodlands p30

A632

Sherwood Forest
Country Park p34

Kirton Wood p33

A60

Ollerton

29

Clay Cross

Mansfield

A617

Sutton in
Ashfield

28

Kirkby in
Ashfield

Alfreton

27

Ripley

Hucknall

MAP 4 ▼ (see p80)

A38

A46

17

MAP 1

Longdendale Estate
Stalybridge

From A57 in Glossop, take B6105 and follow road alongside reservoirs to car park and National Park information centre at Torside. (SK008975)
655lha (16190acres) AONB
United Utilities

A small corner of the vast Longdendale Estate, the fairytale quality of Wildboar Clough makes it a wonderful place to take children. Here you'll find a remnant of the oak and birch woodland that once covered much of the Peak District.

Something of a rarity, the woodland is particularly interesting as well as attractive, with a path winding uphill between stunted oaks and boulders, while a small stream cascades down the rock-strewn ravine. It is a great place to explore and enjoy the views across the reservoirs and moorlands beyond.

Within the small and quickly explored woodland there are more open areas, which add to the interest.

Entry is via the well-surfaced Longendale Trail, part of the Trans-Pennine Trail, which is suitable for wheelchair use although the woodland itself is not. The woodland path climbs up the side of the clough to an open moor where vegetation includes bracken, heather and bilberry. The route is not difficult but boots are recommended.

Shire Hill
Glossop

From Glossop take A57 Snake Pass. Turn left before leaving Glossop into Woodcock Grove signposted Pyegrove Estate and Shire Hill. Follow road to car park and footpath leading to wood. (SK048944) 30ha (73acres) AONB
Peak District National Park Authority

Shire Hill is something of a tranquil gem in the heart of an urban area. A drive through a housing estate to a car park and children's play area is followed by a walk across a football field and then up a steep, uneven narrow path on the edge of another housing estate.

But once you enter the wood, the environment quickly changes, for this ancient woodland of birch and oak has a lovely atmosphere, particularly when bathed in afternoon sun. Trees cover the side of the hill and it feels safe and quiet, ideal for local walks or a short visit after crossing the Pennines. The Trans-Pennine cycle route runs to the north of the wood along the Roman road and links to the Pennine Way.

Tracks and small paths meander through the wood, drawing you to the top of the hill where the landscape changes to heathland, with fine views.

Tom Wood
Glossop

Take A626 between Glossop and Hollingworth towards Charlesworth. Wood is off Woodseats Lane. (SJ998930)
11ha (28acres)
Woodland Trust

The steep terrain and largely undeveloped character of Tom Wood make it a rewarding place to explore – with care – and a great destination for those seeking a morning or afternoon trip to the countryside.

The reward is a beautiful landscape with ash, oak, birch and sycamore, often balanced with a good display of varied wild flowers.

The woodland has a truly rural feel, lining the steep sides of a large bowl-shaped valley in the heart of flat farmland. It forms a clear landmark from the surrounding villages, hills and roads, a little surprising given that Manchester is very close by.

The steep slopes can become very muddy so sturdy footwear should be worn, whatever the time of year.

MAP 1

Snake Woodlands
Glossop

Take A57 from Glossop or
Sheffield. Park in Birchin Clough
layby. (SK109915)
152ha (376acres) AONB
Forestry Commission

Woodland trails lead down
steep-sided valleys through
spruce and larch plantations.
The best of these follow the
river which brings welcome
variety to an otherwise
conifer-dominated site.

There are some pleasant
glades along the river with one
leading through an open valley
of moorland vegetation where
you can enjoy a picnic and
the views.

Walking is generally easy-to-
moderate but the steps from
the road to the start of the
trails are fairly steep and care
should be taken on the stone-
surfaced path which can get
slippery when wet.

The blue trail will take
around one-and-a-half hours,
the white trail an hour. Likely
to get muddy after rain, it's
best to go armed with
wellingtons.

Snake Woodlands can form
part of a longer walk to Kinder
Scout, the highest peak in the
National Park.

South Yorkshire
Community Forest

The South Yorkshire Forest is
a mix of open spaces,
woodland, wetland, farmland,
meadow and urban areas,
covering 153 square miles.
The Forest includes the
south of Barnsley, takes in
most of Rotherham and the
north, south and east of
Sheffield. It aims to make
access to the countryside
easier for all, develop green
links to connect the urban
areas with the countryside
and protect and create areas
for wildlife.

For more information on
Community Forests, see
contact details on page 105.

Upper Derwent Woodlands
Sheffield

Visitor centre is off A57 west of Sheffield. (SK173893)
814ha (2012acres) AONB SSSI
Severn Trent Water

Anyone wishing to see how mature conifer plantations can be managed to create attractive woodland environments would be well advised to visit the Upper Derwent Woodlands.

Commercially managed, the large swathes of woodland surrounding the reservoirs are dominated by conifers but much of this is mature and well thinned – creating a pleasant walking environment.

Facilities throughout the valley are excellent, including the visitor centre at Fairholmes where the feeding station provides a wonderful opportunity to view woodland birds.

Three waymarked trails start out from Fairholmes but those who prefer can plan their own exploration of the site along a good network of footpaths.

Open moorland and reservoir shores are also there to be discovered. Interestingly the dams were used as practice areas by the famed 'Dambusters' during the Second World War – more information is provided in a museum at the west side of Derwent Dam.

MAP 1

Bluebell Wood
New Mills

On A6015 in Hayfield turn into Station Road and left into Hayfield village car park. From A624 follow signs for Sett Valley Trail.
(SK035869) 4ha (10acres) AONB
Derbyshire County Council

As its name suggests, this small, intimate and accessible wood is notable for its carpet of bluebells. A perfect spot to take young children for a spring visit and an interesting diversion for Sett Valley Trail walkers.

The wood features mixed broadleaves including oak, ash, beech and sycamore, with alder and crack willow in its wetter, western end. You'll encounter the glowing, golden flowers of lesser celandine, yellow pimpernel and marsh marigold in the wetter parts.

It's great for birdsong, though don't expect to see them in large numbers. Green and great spotted woodpeckers, nuthatch, willow warbler and chiffchaff have all been recorded here with kingfishers and dippers on the River Sett nearby.

A narrow winding path provides an interesting route through the wood, past a small stream and pond.

Bluebells adding their spring colour

Bitholmes Wood
Sheffield

Woodland straddles A6102
Sheffield to Huddersfield road just
north of Oughtibridge and south
of Stocksbridge. (SK293965)
33ha (82acres)
Woodland Trust

Once part of a large hunting
forest and later a focus for
mining, quarrying and
industrial activity, today
Bitholmes Wood is subject to
little disturbance.

The semi-natural ancient
woodland lies on steep valley
sides, sandwiched between
Sheffield and the Peak District
National Park, and is home to
many bird species, including
woodpeckers and pied
flycatchers.

Limited parking facilities
keep visitor numbers low but
for those who do make it,
there is an attractive circular
walk. Adventurous walkers
who climb to the top end of
the wood are rewarded with
fine views across the Don
Valley.

Once a sessile oak woodland
overlooking the valley, the site
is now dominated by
sycamore, although there
remain large areas of ancient
mixed woodland, particularly
along the crags in the upper
reaches of the wood.

The lower wood still has a
strong ancient woodland feel,
with lots of associated ground
flora, including bluebell, dog's
mercury, wood mellick, wood
millet and cow wheat.

MAP 1

Wharncliffe Woods
Sheffield

Follow signs for Grenoside village from A61. Head north out of village along Woodhead Road. (SK324951) 456ha (1127acres)
Forestry Commission

Robust scenery, open moorland, steep terrain and streams make a delightful backdrop for Wharncliffe and nearby Wheata (see below) and Greno woods – an enjoyable family outing destination.

Part of the South Yorkshire Forest, the woodland has an interesting history. Wharn is a corruption of quern, a handmill used for grinding grain. In medieval times

Wharncliffe Chase was part of a royal hunting park and more recently coal and gannister were mined here. In Greno woods, stone was mined for buildings.

You'll find traces of all these activities in the mix of woodland and fields. Though much of the area was planted with conifers after the Second World War, signs of ancient oak and birch woodland are everywhere.

Greno Wood features areas of Corsican pine and extensive heathland with ling, bilberry, broom and gorse. Birch and oak are regenerating here.

All-terrain bikers, horse riders and walkers all get a fair share of access routes, though most are generally strenuous.

Wheata Woods
Sheffield

Follow signs for Grenoside village from A61. Head north out of village along Woodhead Road. (SK328943)
55ha (136acres)
Sheffield City Council

The site is made up of three neighbouring woods: Wheata, Prior Royd and Birkin Royd. Part of an extensive wooded area, these are distinctive from other local woods, being largely semi-natural ancient woodland.

Rich in ground flora, wildlife and bird species, it has been designated a local nature reserve. Much is also a scheduled ancient monument, featuring the remains of a Romano-British settlement.

Wheata Wood, the largest of the three, is open, flat and easy to access, even with wheelchairs. Prior Royd is a denser wood with more steep slopes, while Birkin Royd clothes the steep sides of a stream valley and is the most difficult to access.

Oak and birch trees dominate but you'll also discover alder in the wetter areas plus beech, sweet chestnut, sycamore and conifers.

Sweet Chestnuts

Rivelin Valley
Sheffield

From A61 at Owlerton take A6101. Follow road over B6079 towards Malinbridge. Wood on right once through Malinbridge. (SK324888)

100ha (247acres)

Sheffield City Council

Forming a green corridor stretching towards the Peak District, the Rivelin Valley provides wonderful riverside walks where you can spot dipper and heron.

Until the 20th century, the river was used to power grinding mills. Ample evidence of the area's industrial heritage can be seen along your walk, in the form of dams, mill-ponds and weirs.

The main path along the valley is suitable for the majority of users but it can get muddy, even boggy, in wet weather.

MAP 1

Ecclesall Woods
Sheffield

On A621 turn west at Beauchief
traffic lights onto Abbey Lane.
(SK323824)
140ha (346acres)
Sheffield City Council

Ecclesall Woods is the largest
ancient woodland site in the
Sheffield area and has a
wonderful array of wildlife.

Spring visitors can enjoy the
dazzling sight of carpets of
bluebells on the woodland
floor and the keen eyed might
even spot all three British
native woodpecker species –
the great spotted, lesser spotted
and green woodpecker.

Exploration is made possible
thanks to an extensive network
of public footpaths and
bridleways and walking
conditions are generally very
good. There is a special trail for
the less able.

There is a lot to discover
including charcoal hearths, a
wood collier's grave, old
coppice stools and some
magnificent stands of old beech.

Padley Gorge
Grindleford

B6521 to Grindleford and park at
rail station. (SK251789)
25ha (62acres) AONB SSSI
National Trust

The ancient woodland that lies
against the dramatic backdrop
of Padley Gorge is recognised
as being one of the best sessile
oak woods in the south
Pennines.

It makes a great family
destination, contrasting with
the classic limestone gorge and
woodland at Dovedale.

This site boasts an interesting
history. The gritstone used to
be quarried for millstones from
which the area gets its name
and can be seen next to the
path at the top end of the
wood, southeast of the river.

Walking through the site is
generally easy, though the top
of the woodland can be more
difficult. Some paths are stone-
surfaced which can get muddy
and slippery – so walking
boots are advised.

For a good picnic spot, take
the circular walk from
Grindleford Station along the

Padley Gorge

riverside, cross the footbridge
to the open country above the
woodland. Cross down to the
other side of the gorge where
the cool, shady woodland
contrasts with the open
moorland.

27

MAP 1

Nor Wood, Cook Spring & Owler Car
Dronfield

Take A61 south from Sheffield for 8km (5 miles) then left onto B6056 to Eckington. Left into Owler Car Lane and entrance 30m down lane on left.
(SK371805)
31ha (76acres) SSSI
Woodland Trust

There's a rural feel to Nor, Cook Spring and Owler Car woods. It's not surprising local residents enjoy relaxing here.

The woods form part of a larger complex that includes Coalpit Wood, Newfield Spring Wood and Whinacre Wood and has a long history of human use. Once surface-mined, the area was cleared and replanted with non-native species – larch, red oak, maple and sycamore. But there is still a good year-round variety of flora and fauna including ferns, bluebells, dog's mercury and barren strawberry, which loves hedge-banks and clearings. Today most trees are native including oak and ash high forest with a wild cherry, holly and hazel understorey.

Part of Cook Spring Wood has Site of Special Scientific Interest (SSSI) designation as one of Derbyshire's most unchanged oak woods.

Owler Car once had some 25 white coal hearths, hinting that lead smelting may have taken place during the last century. Coppice stools suggest charcoal burning also took place here.

Burrs Wood
Unthank

Take B6051 to Milthorpe and turn off to Unthank. Entrance just through Unthank on right.
(SK305755)
13ha (33acres)
Woodland Trust

Scenic and largely unspoilt, Burrs Wood is a peaceful place to explore, despite its proximity to Sheffield and Chesterfield, both of which lie just 10 miles away.

This ancient woodland covers the valley sides of a small stream on the edge of the Peak District National Park.

Oak dominates and some of the more mature specimens are probably well over 200 years old. There is also birch, rowan, a scattering of ash, elder and, near the roadside, elms. Enormous tree stumps indicate regular coppicing once took place here. Conifers were planted in the late 19th century but today only larch remains.

Burrs Wood has an abundance of attractive and well-loved wild flowers including bluebells, wood-sorrel, creeping jenny, ramsons and meadowsweet.

Stand Wood
Bakewell

Follow brown signs to Chatsworth, north of Matlock off B6012.
(SK259702)
96ha (237acres) AONB
Chatsworth Estate

Stand Wood at Chatsworth is a 19th-century romantic-landscape adventure playground that is still delighting visitors in the 21st century. The real 'pièce de résistance' is a man-made dell with an elaborate waterfall.

This is a well-managed woodland with both timber and aesthetic value. The site is a mixture of young pine and beech hilltop plantations contrasting with the main areas of mature beech and oak, with sections of yew, elm and holly.

Surfaced roads and waymarked tracks wend their way through the wood, which is generally fine for all ages and fitness levels but the terrain can be quite steep.

Rocky outcrops provide consistent reminders that the wood is in the heart of the gritstone Peak.

The waymarked main paths could be used as part of an enjoyable longer walk between Baslow and Beeley.

MAP 1

Linacre Woodlands
Chesterfield
Located off B6050 west of Cutthorpe. (SK335728)
81ha (200acres)
Severn Trent Water

Linacre Woodlands

Everyone, from grandparents to tots, can find something to enjoy in Linacre Woodlands, be it the woodland mix, its three reservoirs, multitude of wildlife or the regular events.

This is a very popular site but large enough not to look crowded, and served by a series of well-laid-out car parks nestling in pockets of woodland. Display boards at each car park highlight the series of walks and circular routes that can be enjoyed around the reservoirs.

The woods themselves are a mixture of conifers – larch and pine concentrated on the southern fringe – and broadleaves such as oak, beech, ash, birch and holly.

A demonstration area has been created where seasonal aspects of woodland management are explained. On path edges a number of information boards describe the site's history.

The woodland attracts a wide variety of wildlife and there is usually a warden on hand to point out aspects of seasonal interest.

Walks along well-maintained paths follow the valley upstream, changing to boardwalks in spots where the path cuts into the water's edge. They lead to the top end of the site which tends to be the quietest and you can enjoy excellent views across the valley. Designated a conservation site, cycles are excluded and dogs permitted only when on a lead.

MAP 1

Eaton Wood
Retford

From A638 at Eaton take minor road toward Upton. Wood half-way between Eaton and Upton. (SK727772) 25ha (62acres)

Nottinghamshire Wildlife Trust

Historic Eaton Wood is mentioned in the *Domesday Book* and is worthy of note for its flora – particularly the impressive spring display of bluebells and primroses followed by orchids – and its fairytale quality.

Ancient in origin, it stands on a prominent ridge yet is quietly tucked away and secluded, despite its proximity to the A1. The silence is usually punctuated only by the sound of the London to Edinburgh mainline railway.

Low-key but well-marked paths lead through a variety of habitats including thinned and newly coppiced areas where you may even see charcoal being made.

The main tree species are oak, ash, birch and sycamore with planted beech and conifers, which are gradually being removed. There is a dense understorey of hawthorn, blackthorn and field maple providing wildlife shelter. You might spot a deer or disturb a woodcock.

Clumber Park
Worksop

Follow A614 off A1 and take first turning on right at Apleyhead Lodge. (SK645773) 539ha (1332acres) SSSI

National Trust

An incomparable double avenue of limes greets you – stunning in summer or winter and exceptional in spring.

A good number of interesting trails take you through the heath, birch and oak woodland and conifer plantations that make up the site, which features a year-round programme of events.

Most people are drawn to the lake. An excellent circular walk takes in a variety of sights and habitats. On the southern shore, work is underway to clear rhododendron and open up views to an assortment of follies, ruins and a slightly forbidding Gothic revival chapel. Surrounding this is a mini-arboretum.

Cyclists are encouraged to use the park via a good network of cycle routes and bikes can be hired on site. Alternatively, explore quieter sections from a network of paths and bridleways. Also worth a visit is the newly refurbished organic kitchen garden.

Clumber Park

Kirton Wood
Ollerton

From A6075 take road to Egmanton. Wood halfway between Kirton and Egmanton. (SK707687) 20ha (49acres) SSSI

Nottinghamshire Wildlife Trust

One of the striking features of Kirton Wood is the uniform size of the trees – the result of the site being cleared half a century ago.

Bought by the Wildlife Trust in 1985, the ash and wych elm wood is a designated Site of Special Scientific Interest (SSSI) and is also rich in hazel,

hawthorn, field maple and dogwood.

Flowers such as wood anemone, sweet woodruff, primrose, ramsons, yellow archangel and early-purple orchid confirm its ancient status. You can also find common spotted and butterfly orchids, and bluebells.

Visitors can take advantage of guided walks around the site – by arrangement – to explore the variety of rides and look out for butterflies such as common blue, brimstone, orange tip and comma – or birds like the sparrowhawk, blackcap, spotted flycatcher and great spotted woodpecker.

MAP 1

Sherwood Forest Country Park
Ollerton or Edwinstowe

Signposted from M1 and A1 with brown tourist signs. Follow B6034, north of Edwinstowe. (SK626678)

181ha (447acres) SSSI

Nottinghamshire County Council

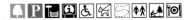

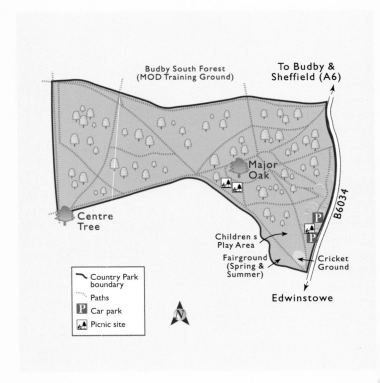

Sherwood Forest Country Park

Any child who has dreamed of Robin Hood and his famous haunts in Sherwood Forest couldn't fail to be delighted by the modern day Sherwood Forest Country Park.

It simply has all the ingredients you need for a great family day out – including the famous Major Oak, Birkland ancient oak wood and even the men in green themselves!

Good visitor facilities, ample car parking, a fun programme of events in the summer and excellent information all add to the Sherwood Forest experience. But there is so much more to be derived from visiting this area, and children are quick to tap into their own imaginations as they explore this ancient woodland.

Well-surfaced paths radiate from the centre, including a round trip for those making the 'pilgrimage' to the Major Oak.

As you explore the woodland you become aware of vast numbers of gnarled veteran oak trees (996 at the last count) which are carefully monitored yet allowed to retain a wild and eerie quality.

If you venture away from the marked paths you will enter heathland, developing woodland and a patchwork of scrub and rough grassland, which creates an area rich in invertebrate species. Birds recorded on site include crossbill, long-eared owl, sparrowhawk, redstart, nightjar and all three British native woodpecker species.

A number of footpaths cross the area, including a medium distance walk called the 'Robin Hood Way' while cyclists can take the Sustrans cycle route to access Clumber in the north or Sherwood Pines in the south (see next entry).

MAP 2

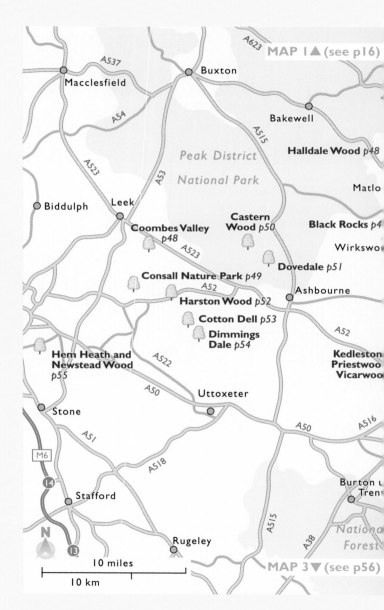

MAP 1▲ (see p16)

A623

A537

Macclesfield

Buxton

Bakewell

A54

A515

Peak District

Halldale Wood *p48*

A523

A53

National Park

Matlo

Biddulph

Leek

Castern
Wood *p50*

Black Rocks *p4*

Coombes Valley
p48

Wirkswo

A523

Dovedale *p51*

Consall Nature Park *p49*

A52

Harston Wood *p52*

Ashbourne

Cotton Dell *p53*

A52

Dimmings
Dale *p54*

Kedleston
Priestwoo
Vicarwoo

Hem Heath and
Newstead Wood
p55

A522

A50

Uttoxeter

A516

Stone

A50

A51

A518

Burton u
Tren

M6

14

A515

Stafford

A38

N

Rugeley

Nationa
Forest

13

10 miles

MAP 3▼ (see p56)

10 km

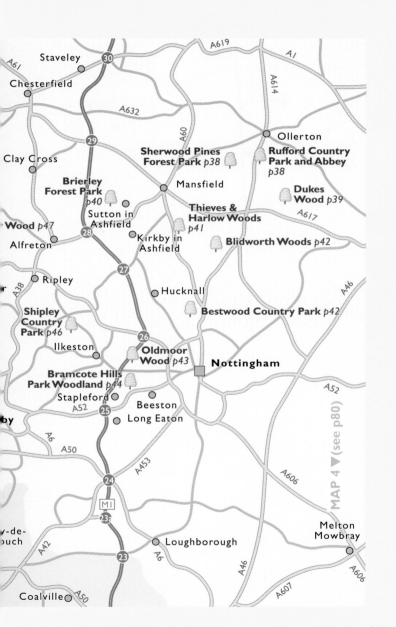

Staveley

A61

Chesterfield

A619

A1

A614

30

A632

29

A60

Clay Cross

Sherwood Pines
Forest Park p38

Ollerton

Rufford Country
Park and Abbey
p38

Brierley
Forest Park
p40

Mansfield

Dukes
Wood p39

Wood p47

Sutton in
Ashfield

Thieves &
Harlow Woods
p41

A617

Alfreton

28

Kirkby in
Ashfield

Blidworth Woods p42

A38

Ripley

27

A46

Hucknall

Bestwood Country Park p42

Shipley
Country
Park p46

A46

Ilkeston

26

Oldmoor
Wood p43

Nottingham

Bramcote Hills
Park Woodland p44

A52

Stapleford

25

Beeston

by

A52

A6

A50

Long Eaton

24

A453

A606

MAP 4 ▼ (see p80)

M1

23

y-de-
ouch

A42

Melton
Mowbray

Loughborough

23

A6

A46

A607

A606

Coalville

A50

37

MAP 2

Sherwood Pines Forest Park
Mansfield

Situated off B6030 east of Old Clipstone. (SK612646)
1200ha (3000acres)
Forestry Commission

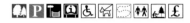

Sherwood Pines is the East Midlands' largest open-access wood. It is dominated, as the name suggests, by pines with just pockets of birch, oak and beech. First impressions of the site are of a well-maintained and organised woodland.

Mainly used by cyclists, (bikes can be hired) this is a working wood with a host of recreational and associated facilities, and visitors are kept well informed thanks to some excellent interpretation and informative maps.

There are lots of glades and open areas throughout the wood. Children with a sense of adventure can explore the site to make their own discoveries or take part in a programme of organised play. You may even be lucky enough to glimpse fallow deer under the trees or hear rare nightjars above the heather at dusk.

Rufford Country Park and Abbey
Ollerton

2 miles south of Ollerton off A614. (SK643652)
40ha (99acres) SSSI
Nottinghamshire County Council

The woodland is just a small – but enjoyable – part of any visit to Rufford Country Park and Abbey, which is popular throughout the year.

There are plenty of tranquil spots to be found in and around the grounds of the former Cistercian abbey, which now houses a cafe, restaurant, garden centre and arts-and-crafts venue where activities take place year-round.

Explore beyond the abbey and its stables and you discover an arboretum with formal gardens containing some interesting sculptures, one of which – a concrete bench framed by a farmer with a ram – is a particular favourite with children.

Rufford Country Park and Abbey

Well-marked and laid paths lead through expanses of grass where rare breeds of sheep wander, to ornamental lakes that culminate in a weir and jetties. The woodland, with holly and yew and other species associated with Sherwood Forest, is reached by well-marked, surfaced paths with points of interest highlighted.

Dukes Wood
Newark

Entrance to reserve off minor road to Eakring, which leaves the A617 near Kirklington. (SK675603) 8ha (20acres) SSSI

Nottinghamshire Wildlife Trust

It's fascinating to think that this beautiful reserve stands on the site of what was the UK's first onshore oilfield – where some 280,000 tons of oil have been extracted.

On this unique site the area's industrial heritage can be appreciated whilst enjoying ▶▶

39

MAP 2

its natural background too –
for today it is a mixed
deciduous woodland.
Dominant trees are oak, ash,
hazel and birch with guelder
rose, dogwood, wild privet and
elder beneath. You may be
lucky enough to spot blackcap,
spotted flycatcher and jays, or
hear the tapping of the great
spotted woodpecker. While
resident red deer, fox and stoat
are rarely seen there are

butterflies aplenty.

Some of the 'nodding
donkeys' – pumps that worked
the oilfield – have been
restored and can be seen close
to a specially created industrial
archaeology nature trail called
the Dukes Wood Trail.

There is a small information
centre documenting the
history and development of the
site, and a leaflet describing
highlights found on the trail.

Brierley Forest Park
Sutton-in-Ashfield

Main entrance and car park on
Skegby Road, Huthwaite, near
M1/A38 junction. (SK476600)
100ha (247acres)

Ashfield District Council

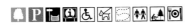

Nurtured as a young section of
the Greenwood Community
Forest, Brierley Forest Park has
been moulded from former
colliery land, farmland and
council playing fields into an
extensive mosaic of landscaped
habitats.

Some 80,000 trees were
planted in the mid 1990s, and a
new lake, wetlands and wild

flower meadows were created.
Set on one of the highest
points in Nottinghamshire, the
site also provides some
stunning views over the
surrounding countryside.

Everyone has been catered
for at Brierley Forest.
Extensive, well-marked routes
are provided for walkers,
cyclists, riders and the less able
and there are nature
conservation areas, art and
recreation facilities and a useful
visitor centre. A recent addition
to the site is a sculpture trail.

The area's rich history –
linked with coal mining,
railways and agriculture – adds
an interesting dimension to
your visit.

Thieves & Harlow Woods
Mansfield or Kirkby in Ashfield

Two car parks off B6139. Third car park at Portland Training College provides access from A60.
(SK552567) 147ha (363acres)
Forestry Commission

Now part of Greenwood Community Forest, Thieves Wood was once part of the Royal Wood of Lyndhurst. Its name is thought to have come from the activities of highwaymen who preyed on travellers heading north on the King's Way.

Today it remains a hive of activity, but the emphasis is on walking, riding and picnicking. The woodland boasts an array of paths and tracks covering undulating terrain. One of the longer trails follows the route of the King's Way, linking the car park with the visitor centre.

Harlow Wood is a quieter setting. Surrounding Portland Training College, it is well used by local residents for riding, walking and exercising their dogs and many people enjoy a stop in the small college tea room as a reward after a long walk.

The site has a short surfaced route, suitable for the less able.

Greenwood Community Forest

Nottinghamshire's Community Forest, the Greenwood covers vast swathes of the county, where a working partnership is providing a greener setting close to the homes of more than a million people.

Covering 160 square miles, it links historic Sherwood Forest in the northeast with Attenborough in the southwest. The forest itself incorporates a host of smaller woods and landscapes – including Brierley Forest Park, Foxcovert Plantation, Bestwood Country Park and Burntstump Country Park, along with Colliers Wood, Dob Park, Moor Pond and Dams Bank Wood, Portland Park Local Nature Reserve, Vicar Water Country Park, Bulwell Hall Park and Thieves and Harlow Woods.

MAP 2

Blidworth Woods
Blidworth
Located west off A614
Nottingham to Doncaster road.
Woods accessed from A614 along
Longdale Lane. (SK597545)
400ha (989acres)
Forestry Commission

Romantics will love the fact
that Blidworth Woods, in the
very heart of the old Royal
Forest of Sherwood, still
contain echoes of their historic
origins, through its ancient
oaks and remnant heathland.

The woods include Sansom
and Haywood Oaks as well as
Blidworth and provide a
variety of walks ranging from a
short, surfaced trail suitable for
wheelchair users and cyclists to
longer cross-country hikes, all
offering much of interest.

A waymarked trail linking the
three car parks allows easy
exploration – and it's possible
to join the Robin Hood Way,
linking Thieves Wood beyond
(see previous page).

A horse-box park is provided
at Blidworth Bottoms car park,
from where you can access a
network of waymarked bridle
tracks. Please note, riders must
have a permit.

Bestwood Country Park
Nottingham
Access from Park Road, off
Bestwood Road (B683) and A611
or Bestwood Lodge Drive near
B6004. (SK565474)
260ha (643acres)
**Nottinghamshire County Council
and Gedling Borough Council.**

Once part of Sherwood Forest
and now part of the extensive
Greenwood Community
Forest, Bestwood Country
Park is a site steeped in
history.

Originally a royal hunting
preserve used by a large
number of English monarchs,
the estate was acquired by Nell
Gwynne in 1687. A medieval
hunting lodge once stood on
the site of Victorian-built
Bestwood Lodge.

By 1939, with the golden age
of English country estates
over, the estate was sold off but
today the 650 acres that form
the country park are a
recreational magnet for

thousands of people.

An array of habitats – from woodland and wetland to wildflower meadow and reedbed – hosts thousands of species. This is thought to be the county's richest site for fungi, with more than 200 species recorded. Guided walks, events, courses and conservation projects are organised throughout the year.

Oldmoor Wood
Nottingham

A610 east towards Nottingham, turn right onto A6002 to Strelley. Park in village. Wood is accessed down a country lane 200m north of church. (SK499420)

15ha (38acres)

Woodland Trust

Considering Nottingham city centre is a mere five miles away, Oldmoor Wood lies in a surprisingly rural area, part of an undulating landscape of farmland, hedgerows and small woods.

The wood itself is mainly flat with an attractive combination of high forest and open glades with dense scrub along the southwest boundary. A network of tracks form easy circular walks through the wood. There is a good variety of trees, the dominant canopy being oak, ash, sycamore and beech with an understorey including holly, rowan, blackthorn and hawthorn.

Bluebells, dense in patches, are scattered throughout the wood where you can also find wood anemone, wood-sorrel, lesser celandine and creeping jenny. Within the wood is a small circular pond, with beautiful old yews standing on its central island.

MAP 2

Bramcote Hills Park
Nottingham

Take A6007 Ilkeston road east
from major roundabout on A52.
Follow signs for Ilkeston for 800m
(0.5 mile) and car park on right.
(SK499384)
7ha (16acres)
Broxtowe Borough Council

A great place to escape the
city, Bramcote Hills Park
offers some great informal
woodland walks, gardens and
an historic hall.

From the car park choices are
varied – a trim trail, an all-
abilities path to the hall and
restored walled gardens, or
more vigorous walks up a steep
hill to the woodland.

More adventurous visitors
will be tempted by the lure of
the uphill walks, with the
reward of some excellent views
across Nottingham and
surrounding countryside. It's a
good place to get away from
the crowds and enjoy
tranquillity.

The nearby walled gardens
are delightful and feature a
touching Holocaust memorial
garden and a human sundial
that will delight children.

Just over the busy minor
road, it's worth visiting
Broxtowe Borough Council's
Hemlockstone open space
and woodland.

Kedleston Hall, Priestwood & Vicarwood
Derby

National Trust signposts from A38.
(SK313404) 354ha (874acres)
National Trust

The approach to Priestwood
and Vicarwood, along an
elegant drive, provides an
impressive introduction to the
park, with constantly changing
panoramic views of veteran
trees, roundels, lakes and a
magnificent neo-classical hall.
The parkland was laid out by
Robert Adam, designer of
Kedleston Hall.

Its boundary woods, the
parkland with veteran oak and
beech, lakes and the Pleasure
Ground, landscaped in the
1760s, will add variety to your
visit. A number of stately
veteran oaks are scattered across

Kedleston Park

the park, both in avenues and informal groups. Evidence of a ha-ha can be seen between the grassland and woodland.

The woods vary from oak, lime, beech, ash, horse chestnut and yew to a younger plantation of pine and the occasional veteran beech and oak. Where the wood meets the lake edge there is a new beech maze.

The park is open to the public between March and December.

MAP 2

Shipley Country Park
Heanor

Take A608 from Heanor to
Smalley. Turn left into Heanor Gate
Industrial Park, turn right at the
end to car park. (SK431453)
250ha (600acres)
Derbyshire County Council

Created as part of a pioneering
landscape reclamation
programme by the National
Coal Board in the 1970s,
Shipley Country Park is the
place to go for variety and a
busy all-year-round events
calendar.

Once mines and spoil heaps,
the area now has lots to offer,
from established woods, a
reservoir and wetlands to open
space, a fishing lake and the site
of Shipley Hall with its restored
formal gardens and quirky
water tower.

The information centre has a
wealth of amenities, along with a
wildlife garden and toddlers' play
area – and improvements are
constantly being made. There are
plenty of surfaced paths, but the
going can get muddy so
remember your boots.

If you prefer more tranquil,
established woodland, Shipley
Wood in the eastern corner of
the park fits the bill with oak,
ash and birch. Smaller copses
can be found along Bell Lane
bridleway to the west.

Shipley Country Park

Black Rocks
Cromford

Take B5036 (off A6) south towards Wirksworth. After 1.5km (1 mile) take left hand turn signed Black Rocks. Car park 200m on left. (SK291557)
Forestry Commission

Black Rocks takes its name from the massive gritstone outcrops at the entrance to the site. Popular with climbers, they also provide visitors with impressive views across the Peak District National Park.

Dominated by Corsican and lodgepole pines, the site is easy to explore via well-marked routes from where you might spot small birds such as the goldcrest. Most of the woodland trails lead through the more diverse areas of the site: glades and open areas of heather linking with more mature woodland. Views across the countryside can be gained from a series of vantagepoints along the trails.

Interesting features of the site are old lead mine workings, where mountain pansies thrive on the spoil heaps.

Bow Wood
Lea Bridge

From A6 exit at junction near Cromford take minor road towards Holloway. Wood is before Cromford Mill and Holloway. Park at Lea Bridge. (SK315564)
Woodland Trust

Bow Wood near Matlock is a good example of the semi-natural oak and birch woodland that once cloaked the area.

Set on a sloping site, it faces south and west across the Derwent Valley. At the top of the wood is the Wickey Tor, which offers stunning views towards the Peak District National Park.

Bow Wood is well used by local people walking the Shining Cliffs complex of paths. Here you will discover large beech and sycamore trees towering above bracken, which turns a beautiful golden colour in autumn.

The central field allows much more light into this part of the wood, giving it a very different and striking character.

MAP 2

Halldale Wood
Two Dales
A6 between Bakewell and Matlock,
follow B5057 northeast. At Two
Dales take road to Darley Hilside.
First right and right again at next
junction. Wood on right, reached
via footpath. (SK283643)
21ha (53acres)
Woodland Trust

Set atop the steeply sloping
sides of a valley, Halldale Wood
forms a sizeable slice of the
woodland that straddles
Halldale Brook.

The eastern side of the valley
is a good example of the oak
and birch woodland that once
cloaked the area, and there are
attractive pockets of ash along
the valley floor.

The woodland itself is classed
as semi-natural ancient
woodland, with yew, an ancient
woodland indicator, helping to
confirm its status. Some
sections of the site were
replanted between 1920 and
1973 – predominantly with
mixed broadleaves.

There is a good variety of
ground flora and a large
number of woodland birds to
be discovered throughout
the year.

Visitors are advised to go
prepared with stout footwear.

Coombes Valley
Leek
Follow A523 Leek to Ashbourne
road. After 6.5km (4 miles) turn
left, signed Apesford and RSPB
Coombes Valley. (SK009534)
160ha (395acres) SSSI
RSPB

Coombes Valley is a
wonderfully secluded and
sheltered wooded valley that
contrasts dramatically with the
open, exposed landscape of the
Staffordshire moorlands
through which it runs.

The broadleaved woodland of
oak, birch, holly and beech also
features species-rich streamside
meadows. Up on the higher
ground are open areas of
heather, with bracken and
gorse, enclosed by old dry-
stone walls.

Along the top of the valley
are areas of young broadleaved
woodland, which contrast with
adjacent mature woodland.

Small birds favour the woodland edges. Two hides, one overlooking a pond and the other in the treetops, provide the chance to see a variety of birdlife from heron to woodpecker.

Consall Nature Park
Cheddleton

From A522 turn onto minor road to Consall then left at T-junction in village to Consall Forge. Entrance to park on right. (SJ993485)
94ha (232 acres)
Staffordshire County Council

Lying almost in the shadows of nearby Alton Towers, this lovely, secluded site lies tucked quietly away in the Staffordshire countryside but holds rich rewards for those willing to seek it out.

It is situated in the valley of a River Churnet tributary and makes a wonderful launch pad for exploration of the intimate and sheltered landscape of the steep, wooded valleys.

Oak and birch woodland lines the valley sides, with open glades and fishing ponds on the valley bottom. This varied, mixed woodland comes into its own in spring when it is alive with birdsong.

There are three waymarked trails, including one around the fishing ponds with the chance to glimpse kingfishers. Those willing to explore further along can enjoy spectacular views of the Churnet Valley.

MAP 2

Castern Wood
Leek

From Ilam follow minor road towards Wetton, through Stanshope to T-junction at Hopedale and turn left. 400m turn left and park on right after further 400m. (SK120538)
21ha (51acres) AONB SSSI
Staffordshire Wildlife Trust

Castern Wood is arguably one of the country's finest and most scenic reserves.

Set within the Peak District Dales, Castern is part of the Hamps and Manifold Valley Site of Special Scientific Interest. Recently also designated as a Special Area of Conservation, this recognises its significance.

The reserve has a diverse range of deciduous trees — dominated by oak, ash, hazel and field maple. Small and large-leaved lime are present, indicating the antiquity of the woodland. Over 340 species of plant have been recorded including spring-flowering cowslips and violets followed by orchids and aromatic salad burnet. In the valley meadow you may see the nodding heads of water avens along the banks of the River Manifold in summer. During dry spells the river vanishes, flowing underground and reappearing further downstream at Ilam.

Excellent views can be enjoyed, particularly across the Manifold Valley and Beeston Tor. The valley was mined for lead during the 19th century and several tunnels remain within the reserve.

Dovedale
Ashbourne

Brown tourist sign on A515 just north of Ashbourne. Car park between Thorpe and Ilam, follow signs to Dovedale. (SK145520) 123ha (304acres) AONB SSSI

National Trust

Clear waters running through a deep limestone gorge, dramatic Peak District scenery, rocky outcrops and varied woodland . . . it's not surprising Dovedale is a people magnet.

Such is its popularity you are advised to avoid high season but visit at quieter times when there will be better opportunities to explore.

The River Dove provides the focus throughout an exciting and varied walk. Dippers are common, crayfish less so. Spectacular limestone outcrops add drama with evocative names such as Twelve Apostles, Lover's Leap and Dovedale Church. Caves along the eastern side of the valley delight young visitors.

Within the woodland are rowan, whitebeam and field maple with yew clinging to the rocky outcrops. Grassland areas along the valley support a host of birds and butterflies.

Dovedale

MAP 2

Harston Wood
Cheadle

A52 from Froghall towards
Ashbourne, turn left to Foxt.
Parking 400m on County Council
car park/picnic site. Follow
footpath to reserve boundary.
(SK034479)
18ha (45acres) SSSI
Staffordshire Wildlife Trust

Part of the largest remaining
concentration of woodland in
Staffordshire, Harston Wood
sustains a wonderful variety
of wildlife.

Most of the woodland is
dominated by ash along with
elm, though alder car
predominates along the
valley bottom.

Redstart, wood warbler and
pied flycatcher have been
recorded in the wood along
with great and lesser spotted
woodpecker, nuthatch,
treecreeper, long-tailed tits and
tawny owl.

The rare opposite-leaved
golden-saxifrage can be found
on the valley floor along with
marsh-marigolds and aromatic

Harston Wood

wild garlic, which grows in abundance.

Many woods in the area used to be managed by coppicing but not in recent years. Large numbers of dead and mature trees support a flourishing invertebrate population.

Cotton Dell
Cheadle

Take B5417 from Cheadle towards Oakamoor. County Council car park on right as you enter Oakamoor (SK054449)
64ha (158acres)
Staffordshire Wildlife Trust

Cotton Dell, an area of ancient woodland in the Churnet Valley, is home to a number of unusual species.

The varied woodland of ash, oak, hazel and elm includes less common species such as guelder rose, field maple and bird cherry, while tall alders thrive in wetter spots at the base of the valley. Wild flowers are abundant, with bluebells, wood-sorrel, wood anemone and the uncommon greater woodrush.

Winding through the reserve is Cotton Brook, important for its dramatic rock exposures. Dippers and grey wagtails can often be seen beyond the banks of golden saxifrage and water avens.

Other birds to look out for are the three native species of woodpecker, chiffchaff, warblers and nuthatch.

MAP 2

Dimmings Dale
Cheadle

From Cheadle take B5417 to Oakamoor village, turn right at bottom of steep hill before bridge in village. Take first left and follow narrow lane towards Alton. Car park on left by Ramblers Retreat Cafe. (SK064434)
260ha (643acres) SSSI
Forestry Commission

Dimmings Dale is a spacious ancient woodland site cloaking the sides of the Churnet Valley. In spring the slopes become a misty carpet of bluebells, wood anemones and wood-sorrel while purple foxgloves tower among ferns and bilberries.

The area has a rich industrial heritage and ore-smelting flourished here for 150 years. What was once littered with spoil heaps has developed into a photographer's dream. Scots pine tower above huge rock outcrops, forged in the Ice Age and offering natural resting places along the route of the walk, while large ponds strung along a sparkling stream look like a necklace decorating the valley floor.

Coppicing was the only industry to survive in Dimmings Dale until as recently as the 1950s. Today the lush broadleaved trees provide shelter for a host of creatures including woodpeckers, which can often be heard.

Hem Heath & Newstead Wood
Stoke-on-Trent

South of A5035 between
Trentham and Longton. Car park
east of railway line next to
electricity substation. (SJ885411)
40ha (100 acres)

Staffordshire Wildlife Trust

The largest area of woodland
within Stoke-on-Trent, this is a
green oasis in the industrial
heart of the Potteries.

Bounded by an industrial
estate, main road and railway
line, the urban noise soon fades
as you reach the peace and
tranquillity of an ancient
woodland heart.

Four distinct woodlands make
up the site: Hem Heath and
Newpark Plantation, planted in
the 19th century, contrast with
the ancient woodland of Oaks
and parts of Newstead Wood.

The plantation woods, alive
with a diverse springtime mix
of bluebells, wood-sorrel,
figwort, wood sanicle and
broadleaved hellebore, are easy
to explore via a network of
rides and paths. The oak, ash,
sycamore, beech and cherry
woodland has an open and
attractive feel and a rich
birdlife population including
chiffchaff, willow warbler and
wood warbler.

In contrast, the oak and birch
ancient woodland of the Oaks
and parts of Newstead are
more intimate and secluded,
with a spectacular spring
bluebell display.

MAP 3

Stoke-on-Trent

Newcastle-under-Lyme

A523

A52

Ashbourne

MAP 2 ▲ (see p36)

A52

15

A522

Stone

A50

Uttoxeter

A50

M6

A51

A518

A5

14

Stafford

Battlestead Hill p60

Burton-on-Trent

A515

Natio
Fore

13

Cannock Chase p58

Rugeley

Dunstall Estate p60

A38

A34

George's Hayes p59

Coton Wood p63

12

Cannock

Pipe Hall Farm p58

Lichfield

M6 TOLL

11

2 1

M54

Brownhills

Tamworth

M54

10

10

Walsall

Wolverhampton

9

Sutton Coldfield

N

8 7

M6

9

West Bromwich

6 5

4a 8

10 miles

10 km

Birmingham

4

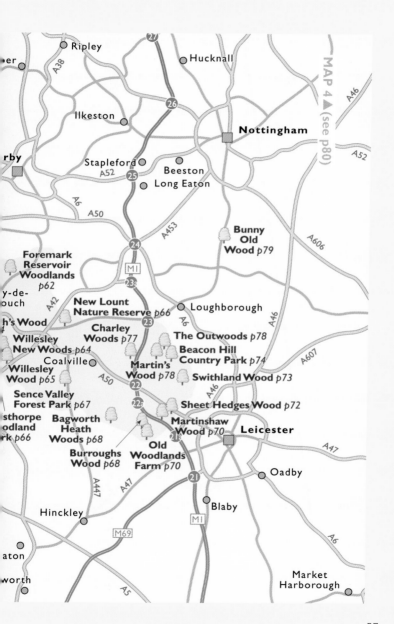

Ripley

er

Hucknall

MAP 4 ▲ (see p80)

Ilkeston

Nottingham

rby

Stapleford
Beeston
Long Eaton

Bunny
Old
Wood p79

Foremark
Reservoir
Woodlands
p62

y-de-
ouch

New Lount
Nature Reserve p66

Loughborough

h's Wood

Charley
Woods p77

The Outwoods p78

Willesley
New Woods p64

Beacon Hill
Country Park p74

Coalville

Martin's
Wood p78

Willesley
Wood p65

Swithland Wood p73

Sence Valley
Forest Park p67

Sheet Hedges Wood p72

sthorpe
odland
rk p66

Bagworth
Heath
Woods p68

Martinshaw
Wood p70

Leicester

Burroughs
Wood p68

Old
Woodlands
Farm p70

Oadby

Hinckley

Blaby

aton

worth

Market
Harborough

57

MAP 3

Cannock Chase
Stafford or Rugely

Take A51 through Rugely. Turn into Hagley Road at traffic lights between the two roundabouts, signposted Cannock Chase Visitor Centre. (SK017171)
65km² (25 sq miles) AONB
Forestry Commission

Cannock Chase is Britain's smallest mainland Area of Outstanding Natural Beauty (AONB), a region of rolling hills covered with lowland heaths and mixed forest. The varied landscape provides stunning contrasts of golden autumn-leaf colour to striking purple heathland.

This area has rich environmental and historical interest – it was once a royal hunting preserve for the Bishops of Lichfield. During the 16th century the woodland was cut for charcoal burning. Long associated with the armed forces, it was also the site of the country's first ever large scale military manoeuvres in 1872.

There are a large number of attractions, among them museums, family cycle routes and a herd of fallow deer.

Many visitors like to start out from the Birches Valley Forest Centre, where there is an excellent shop and an education team.

Pipe Hall Farm
Burntwood

From A461 between Lichfield and Brownhills, take A1590 west towards Burntwood. Take road towards Woodhouses, turn right in village and car park 400m on right. (SK083095) 49ha (120acres)
Woodland Trust

Popular with visitors, who make the most of the flat, easy, enjoyable walking, Pipe Hall Farm lies between the two local communities of Burntwood and Lichfield, in the Mercia Community Forest.

Set within a mainly arable area, much of the site is new plantation, dominated by native broadleaves with a smaller proportion of conifers in open grassland areas.

Two established woods, Parkers Plantation – once part of the Maple Hays Estate – and the Roundabouts, along with an area of rising ground, provide views across the historic parkland landscape that surrounds Maple Hays Hall, to Lichfield Cathedral beyond.

An extensive network of paths run throughout the woodland, giving good access to the entire site.

George's Hayes
Lichfield

On A51 Rugeley to Lichfield road, turn southwest into Borough Lane at Longdon. At T-junction with Horsey Lane, turn left and parking area (Piggot's Bottom) 400m on right. (SK067133) 19ha (48acres)
Staffordshire Wildlife Trust

Renowned for Staffordshire's largest wild daffodil colony, George's Hayes has much to intrigue nature-lovers – despite a chequered history,

Once part of the Beaudesert Estate, which was broken up by the Earl of Anglesey in the 1930s when the land was clear-felled, the site now has few trees over 70 years old.

The reserve, dominated by ash, elm and sycamore, is in fact three woods in one, the nearby woods of Piggott's Bottom and Square Covert neatly complementing George's Hayes.

Piggott's Bottom has a ground flora of daffodils, ramsons, bluebells, red campion, foxgloves and yellow archangel. Beyond a Victorian fishpond lies Square Covert, where red, fallow and Muntjac deer can be seen, along with fox, stoat, badger and water shrew if you're lucky.

Slightly larger, George's Hayes has a rich ground flora including bluebells and lush green carpets of lesser celandine. Among its rarer plants are greater bellflower, tuberous comfrey, broadleaved helleborine and the distinctive wood horsetail.

MAP 3

Dunstall Estate
Barton-under-Needwood

From B5016 between Yoxall and
Barton-under-Needwood take
turn up Forest Road. Small car
park on right at Mosey Mere.
(SK175200) 92ha (227acres)
Dunstall Estate

Exciting work to extend a
beautifully managed
traditional small estate
woodland landscape makes
this a site to watch over
coming years.

Some 100,000 trees and 7km
of hedgerows have been
planted across 49 hectares of
the Dunstall Estate, which lies
on high ground west of the
River Trent, overlooking the
Derbyshire coalfields.

Small woods and plantations
sit among a patchwork of
green fields and open
meadows, including a 30-
hectare area converted from
arable land where field ponds
provide a habitat for wetland
species such as dragonflies.

Invasive sycamores are being
thinned to give oak a chance.
Over the next few years the
character of the landscape will
evolve and interesting
woodland walks will develop.
Access via good paths and
with lovely country views, this
is a place to watch and revisit
again and again.

Battlestead Hill
Tatenhill

From A38 at Burton-on-Trent take
junction to Tatenhill. Track leading
to wood is off first left bend
immediately after leaving A38.
(SK208221) 2ha (6acres)
Woodland Trust

Battlestead Hill is an important
landscape feature within the
Tatenhill Conservation Area.
Mainly mature woodland
with grassland and scrub lying
in a narrow valley, the site is
sandwiched between two new
broadleaf planting schemes –
the 70-acre Bass Millennium
Wood to the northeast and
East Hill Wood, a 45-acre site,
to the west.

A network of rides and paths
links Battlestead with its
fledgling neighbours and a
well-used public footpath
bisects the wood along the

Battlestead Hill

main ride. A circular footpath in the southeast corner is steep in places and can be hard going but is worth it as this area houses earthworks – a series of banks and gullies – believed to be medieval or even earlier in origin.

MAP 3

Foremark Reservoir Woodlands

Swadlincote

A514 at Ticknall follow signpost at end of village. (SK337245) 51ha (126acres) SSSI

Severn Trent Water

A host of activities await you on a visit to Foremark Reservoir, including Carves Rocks.

The reservoir area, which contains a number of interesting wildlife habitats, offers the chance to fish, bird-watch, sail, cycle, or just take a quiet stroll.

The woodland, which stands east of the reservoir, was planted in the 1970s with mainly native species as part of a long-term plan to encourage wildlife conservation and expand amenities. Most of the wood has been planted with oak, rowan, holly and silver birch.

There are some 22 acres of community woodland, with surfaced footpaths concentrated around the visitor centre. Here you can start exploring the magic of the growing National Forest.

National Forest

The National Forest initiative aims to create a new multi-purpose forest covering more than 200 square miles across Leicestershire, Staffordshire and Derbyshire. The Government identified the location for the forest in the early 1990s and established the National Forest Company in 1995. Before work began this was one of Britain's least-wooded landscapes but woodland cover has increased from 6% to over 16%. Linking the two ancient forests of Charnwood and Needwood, the aim is to achieve a patchwork of ancient woodland, new woods, farms, new wildlife habitats, towns and villages, with woodland cover at around 30%. Over 6 million trees have already been planted. 'Conkers', an award-winning attraction at the heart of the National Forest, offers a mix of indoor and outdoor activities for all to enjoy – just 5 miles from junction 11 of the M42 (see p105 for contact details).

Coton Wood
Burton-on-Trent

West off A444 at Overseal,
towards Coton in the Elms. In
village take Little Liverpool Road.
Wood to left of this road.
(SK245145) 33ha (82acres)
Woodland Trust

The past meets the future in
intriguing fashion on a visit to
Coton Wood.

Rich in historic interest, the
site was planted only in 1995
as part of the ever-evolving
National Forest. Since then,
the trees have thrived and
proved popular with local
people who make good use of
the ample access paths.

Chief among some
interesting historical features
is a double hedge and bank,
known as the 'Procession
Way', thought to be the
remnant of an historic lane
used to transport plague
victims during the Black
Death.

The wood boasts 4.7km of
hedges – a mix of neatly
trimmed hawthorn hedges
and overgrown elm and
blackthorn scrub – where,
with some older trees,
wildlife thrives.

The rides and paths provide
experiences for the visitor,
with narrow, dark stretches
and wide, sunny rides. There
is an interesting community
of invertebrates including
small copper and skipper
butterflies, while a variety of
plants thrive in grassland and
scrub conditions.

MAP 3

Sarah's Wood
Moira

Take Measham turn on A42.
Turn right onto B586 toward
Donisthorpe. Carry on to Moira.
Car park 250m north of Moira
crossroads. (SK315158)
12ha (30acres)

Leicestershire County Council

Designed by – and for – the
less abled, Sarah's Wood stands
in the heart of the National
Forest close to the impressive
Conkers activity centre.

A combination of tarmac and
finely crushed stone paths,
provide good access for
wheelchair users (though
assistance is needed in some
sections) and interpretation is
provided at wheelchair level,
where the edges of shrubs have
been cut back to display the
twig colours of species such as
willows and dogwoods. A play
area is also provided.

Below the wood sits the
canal basin, which links with
the Ashby canal and this can
be accessed by all from the car
park at the National Forest
Centre.

Willesley New Woods
Ashby de la Zouch

From Ashby de la Zouch take
B5003 Moira road. At Norris Hill,
turn onto Willesley Woodside and
follow for 1.5km (1 mile) to reach
wood. (SK329156) 24ha (60acres)

UK Coal Mining Ltd

Some of the first trees in the
National Forest are said to have
been planted here.

There are two distinct areas:
the 1990 plantation, and more-
recent planting of alder, ash,
birch and oak. This is a good
place to enjoy views of the
surrounding countryside.

Nearby Shellbrook Wood is
the newer site, with planting
dating from 1998. Part of the
site is dominated by an open-
cast coalface and railhead, an
industrial memento that
reminds us this is a developing
landscape. This wood links
with a footpath to Ashby and
adjacent new planting at
Chestnut Wood.

Willesley Wood
Ashby de la Zouch

Leave A42 at B5006 junction
signposted Ashby de la Zouch.
After 1.5km (1 mile) turn sharp
left, signposted Donisthorpe.
Follow road for 2km (1.5 miles). At
small cross roads turn left into
Willesley Wood. (SK335142)
57ha (141 acres)
Woodland Trust

You will discover Willesley
Wood next to the village of
Donisthorpe, in the heart of
the National Forest.

One of the first to evolve
within Leicestershire's former
coalfield. When mining ended
in 1943 the land was returned
to agricultural use but its
industrial heritage is never far
from view, with visible relics
including nearby Oakthorpe
Colliery.

With new and mature woods,
wetlands, wildflower meadows
and the rare majestic black
poplar, over 70 different types
of bird have made Willesley
Wood their home. There are
even ancient woodland
indicators such as bluebells and
dog's mercury. This award–
winning woodland creation site
is one of 20 Woodland Trust
properties in the National
Forest.

Willesley Wood

MAP 3

Donisthorpe
Woodland Park
Donisthorpe

From A42 take B5006 to
Measham. Turn right before town
centre onto B586 to Donisthorpe.
Moira road car park 250m on right
after crossroads. (SK320143)
30ha (74acres)

Leicestershire County Council

The phrase 'multi-purpose
forestry' acquires real meaning
on a visit to Donisthorpe
Woodland Park, a site that's a
delight for adults and for kids.

First planted in 1996 on a
reclaimed colliery tip, some
skilled land profiling has reaped
spectacular results: snaking
paths, steep enough to be
interesting without precluding
access for the less abled, offer
views which open out
impressively. Add the
atmosphere of boats on the
former Ashby canal, currently
being redeveloped, and the
result is magic.

Plans for the woodland have a
strong educational element,
linking in neatly with the
National Forest and Conkers
exhibition centres.

Well-surfaced paths provide
good access throughout the site
and form a seamless walk
through to the Moira Forge
and tea rooms. Walks along the
canal towpath lead to the centre
and nearby Sarah's Wood
(see p64).

New Lount
Nature Reserve
Shepshed

On A42, take A512 turn east and
then first left on B5324 towards
Belton. Take B587 toward
Melbourne and reserve entrance
on left. (SK399185)
20ha (49acres)

Leicestershire County Council

After more than 30 years as a
colliery, a former tip is re-
emerging as New Lount
Nature Reserve, a vibrant
landscape where wildlife
habitats are evolving.

Popular with locals, it
encompasses fragments of
ancient woodland with oak,
ash and birch and in the wetter
parts, alder and willow.

Approached from the site of
the old mine entrance the

reserve is served by bridleways and footpaths, while a circular walk follows the line of the old narrow-gauge rail line that once transported coal around the site. Birch and gorse are colonising the bare ground on its route.

You might spot a woodpecker, tree creeper, goldcrest or chiffchaff and flowers including orchids, scabious, trefoil, stonecrop, vipers bugloss and St John's wort. Around the ponds look for frogs, moorhens, dragonflies and damselflies.

Sence Valley Forest Park
Ibstock

Take A447 north from Ibstock. Main entrance on left 800m (0.5 mile) north of village. (SK404113) 60ha (148acres)

Leicestershire County Council

Part community forest, part country park, Sence Valley Forest Park is a spectacular example of a dynamic evolving landscape and shows how good design can transform derelict land into a natural asset.

The woodland is tucked away off the Ravenstone Road north of Ibstock and it is not until you leave your car and walk towards the entrance that the impact of the project hits home. It is then that the breathtaking view of the valley below opens up to you.

The network of paths enables walkers, cyclists and riders alike to get the most from a visit without posing a risk to nesting birds. The paths are suitable for pushchairs and the rustic sculptures encountered en route are a delight to young and old. That's not surprising, as children were involved in the woodland design, including the zigzag path that leads up the steepest gradient.

MAP 3

Bagworth Heath Woods
Coalville

Take B585 south from Coalville
through Bagworth village
continuing towards Marylees. Car
park on left immediately past lakes.
(SK456068) 75ha (185acres)
Leicestershire County Council

Here is an excellent
opportunity to see a landscape
in the process of development
– a large, newly planted
woodland created on the site
of a former colliery.

The wood is easy to explore,
via a track leading north and a
well-surfaced circular path to
the south. The gentler southern
route leads to a demonstration
area where you can view dry-
stone walling, pollarding and
sculpture displays.

Heading north you'll discover
a series of ponds laid out for
fishing, with a pair of resident
swans. The central island is
topped with a pit wheel from
the former colliery.

Beyond it are patches of open
ground – good for skylarks –
dotted with smaller pockets of
woodland. Oak and ash are
being planted on the fertile
arable soils. Pine, alder, maple
and poplar in the less fertile
areas. Trials are currently
underway to see how well
these different species are
progressing.

Burroughs Wood
Ratby

From A46 follow signs for Ratby
and Groby. After entering Ratby
take right turn into Burroughs
Lane. Wood 800m (0.5 mile) on
right. (SK492062) 37ha (91acres)
Woodland Trust

Burroughs Wood is a 'wood of
two halves', both of them large
sites and linked via a public
right of way.

The northern section is a
broadleaved woodland with
ancient origins, proving a draw
in the spring when the
woodland floor is awash with
bluebells. South of this is a
newly planted woodland,
created in 1996 and 1997, with
native broadleaf species such as
silver birch with its distinctive
white bark and pale-green
leaves, and hawthorn, whose
heavily scented flowers appear

in May and early June.

There are also remnant hedgerows and open meadows which are cut annually for hay – good news for increasing the range of flora and fauna of the area.

This is a well-used site, particularly along the public and permissive bridleways. Getting around is easy on gentle and undulating slopes.

Burroughs Wood

MAP 3

Old Woodlands Farm
Ratby or Desford

Follow A47 east toward Earl
Shilton. After approx 2km (1 mile)
take B582 signposted Desford.
Approaching Desford take B5380
turn, opposite college. Woods
adjacent to Woodlands Farm.
(SK495052) 10ha (25acres)
Mr F Howitt

Old Woodlands Farm and its
neighbour, Hollow Oak Woods,
are two new sites forming part
of the National Forest.

The younger of the two, Old
Woodlands, has some well-
defined rides leading through
the site, which is framed by
mature hedgerows and a
boundary of ash and oak. On
the southern boundary is a
spring-fed pond.

Holly Oak Wood, is entered
through a shrub-filled hedge,
rich in holly, which has been
allowed to develop as dense
cover for wildlife. It's soon
apparent how the wood got its
name.

From here you can enjoy
excellent views of Ratby
Burrows, an ancient oak and
lime woodland with remnants
of a medieval embankment.

To the west, the Woodland
Trust has undertaken a planting
scheme which, in time, will
become another gem in the
National Forest's crown.

Martinshaw Wood
Groby or Ratby

Turn off A46 at A50 junction and
take turning for Groby, following
signs towards Ratby. At first mini
roundabout after entering Ratby
turn right onto Markfield Road.
Car park 400m on right.
(SK510073)
103ha (255acres)
Woodland Trust

The ancient woodland site of
Martinshaw Wood, on the edge
of the National Forest, features
a variety of species, though
much of its native sessile oak
was replaced with conifers
during the 1950s. The
Woodland Trust, which
acquired the site in 1985, has
the long-term aim of returning
the site to broadleaved
woodland.

The Toothills, a pre-
Cambrian rock outcrop on the

northern boundary, have retained many of the plants associated with semi-natural ancient woodland – helleborine, primrose, wood anemone, wood-sorrel and sanicle.

Martinshaw is also one of the only areas in Leicestershire containing lily-of-the-valley.

Plans for horse and cycle access are in the pipeline.

Martinshaw Wood

MAP 3

Sheet Hedges Wood
Anstey

Entrance on Newton Linford Lane,
off A50 Groby Road. (SK523081)
30ha (75acres) SSSI

Leicestershire County Council

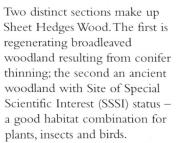

Two distinct sections make up
Sheet Hedges Wood. The first is
regenerating broadleaved
woodland resulting from conifer
thinning; the second an ancient
woodland with Site of Special
Scientific Interest (SSSI) status –
a good habitat combination for
plants, insects and birds.

Marked by a retained fringe of
conifers and ash, the first
section is a good example of
vigorous natural regeneration.
Emerging birch, ash, sallow,
thorn and hazel are
supplemented by planted oak
and ash.

An arable field divides the first
woodland section from its
neighbouring site. Here the
woodland is oak, ash and hazel
with holly, complemented by
regenerating birch, rowan, field
maple and cherry.

Traditional management
methods have been introduced
in sections of the wood and
you might see evidence
of coppicing.

Swithland Wood
Newton Linford

Access off B5330 and from
Woodhouse Eaves. (SK538118)
59ha (146acres) SSSI
Bradgate Park Trust

You will discover Swithland
Wood in the very heart of
ancient Charnwood Forest and,
not surprisingly, there is an
ancient 'feel' to the site. For
example a rocky cove inside
the wood looks like something
straight out of a fairytale.

Extensive yet inviting – and
very busy at weekends – the
woods are mainly oak, birch
and hazel interspersed with the
occasional small-leaved lime,
and areas veer from dense
woodland through dappled
shade to open conditions –
with a few surprises along the
way. It was awarded Site of
Special Scientific Interest (SSSI)
status as the best remaining
example of original oakwood
in the Charnwood Forest.

A number of alder-lined
streams run through Swithland,
adding to its appeal.

There are also unusual
hillocks and pits in the wood
that hint at the quarrying that
once took place here.

Swithland Wood

73

MAP 3

Beacon Hill Country Park
Woodhouse Eaves

14km (9 miles) north of Leicester and 3km (2 miles) south of
Loughborough on outskirts of Woodhouse Eaves. Main entrance on
Breakblock Lane, off Beacon Road. (SK520149)
135ha (334acres) SSSI
Leicestershire County Council

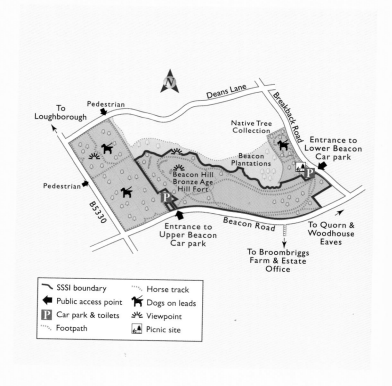

Beacon Hill Country Park

Not only is Beacon Hill Country Park widely recognised as an ecological and archaeological gem, but the 244-metre-high summit is Leicestershire's highest point, offering panoramic views of the county.

The park, owned and managed by Leicestershire County Council, is a huge draw for visitors. Seats allow them to relax and enjoy the scenery and some, made from silver birch trunks, also provide a winter home for small mammals.

The site is made up of mixed woodland, heathland, grassland and farmland. Before and during the Second World War many of the larger trees were lost but specimens of beech, sweet chestnut and Scots pine remain along with native oak and silver birch. A native tree collection has been established close to one of the car parks – the track here is suitable for less-abled visitors – through a planting programme of around 8,000 trees. The collection represents 28 species of tree which became naturally established in Britain after the last Ice Age.

An area of open heathland around the slopes provide an invaluable wildlife habitat and a special programme of nocturnal walks offer the

75

MAP 3

Beacon Hill Country Park

chance to glimpse a fox, tawny owl or one of the three types of bats inhabiting the woodland. If you are lucky you may spot a badger hunting for grubs along the woodland edge.

The site's ecological importance is reflected in the fact that much of it is designated a Site of Special Scientific Interest (SSSI).

Historically this is a fascinating place to visit. Evidence of prehistoric life can be seen through a series of earthworks; the remains of a hillfort dating back as much as 3,000 years to the Bronze Age. Bronze bracelets, axe moulds and spearheads have been discovered on the Beacon Hill, a scheduled ancient monument.

Charley Woods
Whitwick

1.5km (1 mile) northwest of Copt
Oak off the A511. Access to
reserve along track which leaves
the Whitwick Road opposite
Upper Greenhill Farm. (SK476148)
67ha (165acres)

**Leicstershire & Rutland
Wildlife Trust**

Named after nearby Charley
Hall, Charley Woods is actually
made up of three separate
areas; Burrow Wood, Field
Wood and Cat Hill Wood, all
linked by public footpaths.

Burrow Wood is open, with
views of Timberwood Hill to
the west. It is dominated by
oak, with birch, rowan and ash,
hazel and guelder rose. A series
of springs and a stream run
alongside a track, marked by a
thriving line of holly.

The field area has been left to
regenerate naturally and oak
and birch are already
emerging. A pond has been
created in the northeast corner
and natural wetlands lie in the
southeast. Wild flowers such as
lady's smock do well in the
wetter a025eam and higher up
the hill are gorse and broom.

Cat Hill Wood has a subtly
different feel, with a dense
understorey of thorn and holly.

MAP 3

The Outwoods
Loughborough

Following A512 from Loughborough, turn left down Snell's Nook Lane and straight on at Priory traffic lights. Follow Woodhouse Lane for 1.5km (1 mile). Car park on left. (SK515160) 45ha (110acres) SSSI

Charnwood Borough Council

The evocatively named Outwoods has something of a mystical quality. Once part of Charnwood Forest, its rocky outcrops, some lent an orange luminosity by lichen, are unique to this area, hence its Site of Special Scientific Interest (SSSI) status.

At every twist and turn of the woodland, there is something to discover – rare plants, including heath rush and tall sedge, for example – as you are drawn to the centre of a site which has been wooded for centuries. Indeed, records date back to 500AD.

Its eastern boundary features a cluster of ancient oaks that once dominated the forest. Today there are also pine, spruce, larch and younger oak trees. Look out for a plaque, unveiled by the Prince of Wales, commemorating the work of Dr Richard St Barbe Baker who founded 'Men of the Trees'.

The woodland paths are well surfaced and benches are dotted about the site.

Martin's Wood
Woodhouse Eaves

Exit M1 at junction 23. Take A512 west, exiting left onto B591. At crossroads continue straight on. Next left into Deans Lane and wood is on right at top of hill. (SK507152) 5ha (12acres)

Woodland Trust

Martin's Wood in Charnwood Forest stands among the Midland's highest woodland offering spectacular views across the Soar and Trent valleys.

Named after the late president of the Friends of Charnwood, the site was originally gently sloping grassland with two shelterbelts of oak, beech, holly, sycamore and rowan, encompassed by dry stone walls characteristic of the area.

In 1995 the Woodland Trust supplemented this with a programme of planting oak, ash, birch, field maple and a variety of shrubs.

An open area of grassland was retained and this is mown for hay in July to encourage a rich mixture of wild grasses and flowers.

A network of paths and rides provide a circular route, taking in two main vantage points. The public bridleway running alongside the wood gives easy access to Beacon Hill Country Park.

Bunny Old Wood
Keyworth
Main entrance on Bunny Hill off
A60 Loughborough road.
(SK579283)
16ha (40acres)
Nottinghamshire Wildlife Trust

Bunny Wood is an ancient coppiced woodland with a varied and interesting history.

Mentioned in the *Domesday Book*, the site once provided timber for Saxon settlers. Henry VII and his army camped nearby en route to the Battle of East Stoke. Historical evidence of the wood's age can be found in ancient ditches running along the northern and southern edges, and old coppice stools.

Coppiced ash and field maple are a common sight while the southern boundary includes oak, cherry and wild crab apple, along with wood anemone, stitchwort and barren strawberry.

It's rich in wildlife – more than 50 species of bird have been recorded, including the great and lesser spotted woodpecker, and more than 20 butterfly species seen here include the white-letter hairstreak. Some of the dead timber has been retained to encourage woodpeckers, while habitat piles have been built for small mammals, invertebrates and fungi.

MAP 4

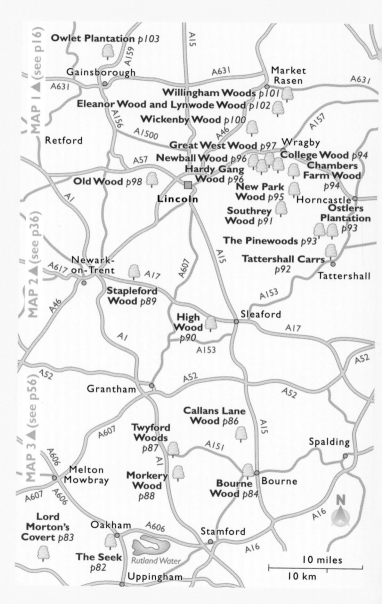

Owlet Plantation *p103*

Gainsborough

A159

A631

A631

A15

A631

Market Rasen

A631

A631

Retford

A156

A1500

A46

A157

Willingham Woods *p101*

Eleanor Wood and Lynwode Wood *p102*

Wickenby Wood *p100*

Great West Wood *p97*

Wragby

A57

Newball Wood *p96*

College Wood *p94*

Hardy Gang Wood *p96*

Chambers Farm Wood *p94*

Old Wood *p98*

Lincoln

New Park Wood *p95*

Horncastle

Southrey Wood *p91*

Ostlers Plantation *p93*

The Pinewoods *p93*

A1

Tattershall Carrs *p92*

Newark-on-Trent

A17

A607

A15

Tattershall

A617

A46

Stapleford Wood *p89*

A153

Sleaford

A17

High Wood *p90*

A1

A153

A52

A52

A52

A52

Grantham

Callans Lane Wood *p86*

A15

Spalding

A607

Twyford Woods *p87*

A151

A1

Morkery Wood *p88*

Bourne Wood *p84*

Bourne

Melton Mowbray

A606

A607

A606

Lord Morton's Covert *p83*

Oakham

A606

Stamford

A16

N

The Seek *p82*

Rutland Water

Uppingham

10 miles

10 km

MAP 1 ▲ (see p16)

MAP 2 ▲ (see p36)

MAP 3 ▲ (see p56)

MAP 4

The Seek
Oakham

Follow A606 through Oakham and take left turn immediately after railway crossing and left again, signed Braunston. Wood 2km (1 mile) on left. (SK839073)

11ha (27acres)

Woodland Trust

Set in a prominent position on the edge of Braunston-in-Rutland and less than two miles from Rutland Water, The Seek has much to offer, not least some stunning panoramic views across beautiful countryside.

This young woodland occupies a prominent southeast slope planted between 1992 and 1994 with oak, ash and hazel.

Local school children were invited to put forward ideas for the design of the woodland, which was appropriately named The Seek, because it is the local name for a 'field running down to a stream'. It has good parking facilities in a layby beside the main entrance.

Development of the woodland is being monitored by the Rutland Natural History Society who have already recorded 20 species of butterfly, 95 species of moth and 64 species of bird on the site.

Common Blue butterfly

Lord Morton's Covert
Leicester

Follow A47 eastwards from Leicester, turning onto B6047 after Billesdon towards Tilton-on-the-Hill. Take left onto minor road 400m before entering village. After 800m, right onto Sludge Hall Hill and wood is on right. (SK723053) 4ha (10acres)

Woodland Trust

A wealth of wildlife thrives in Lord Morton's Covert. Woodcock, tawny owls, green and great spotted woodpeckers are all resident in this sycamore–dominated site.

A key part of the local landscape, the site lies about a mile to the west of Tilton-on-the-Hill, on the north-facing slope of Sludge Hall Hill.

This is a secondary woodland, which was planted as a fox covert in the 19th century on a former ironstone quarry. After its sale in 1960 it was almost completely clear-felled and has since been replanted with stock grown from seed.

Today the wood is predominantly a stand of sycamore high forest. A band of beech runs through the centre while a number of conifers can be spotted, scattered throughout.

A single path provides access, leading from the south of the woodland, directly off Sludge Hall Hill, to the northern end, where the wood is steep and the ground can be very slippery.

MAP 4

Bourne Wood

Bourne

Follow A151 Corby Glen Road from Bourne. Passing A6121 turning, entrance to wood 200m on right. (TF076201)

171ha (423acres)

Forestry Commission

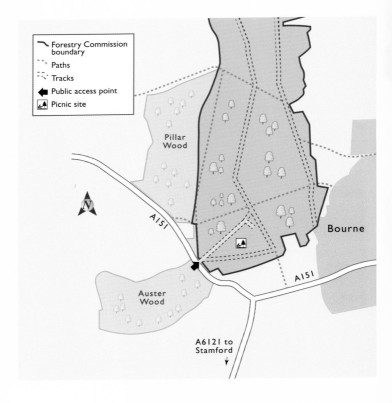

Bourne Wood

There's a magical quality about Bourne Wood, an expansive ancient woodland site that won a Forestry Centre of Excellence Award.

One of its delights is a sculpture trail that is full of surprises ranging from the monumental to the miniature.

A working woodland with a host of interesting facets, Bourne is easy to reach and a pleasure to enjoy, thanks to a generously sized car park, good access, well-planned facilities and a busy summer events programme. Children can make the most of a well-planned play area.

There is a dog-walking trail and access for the less abled leading directly from the car park into the wood, where it is possible to spend hours exploring along the well-surfaced rides.

The site is a patchwork of differing forestry compartments, ranging from coppiced hazel to mature conifers and open grassland. The more determined walker can leave the crowds behind and head for the quieter, more remote corners. The grassland habitats offer a wonderful vantage point for watching butterflies and there are extensive ponds – well worth a visit.

MAP 4

Callans Lane Wood
Bourne

Leave A15 Bourne to Sleaford road at crossroads for Kirkby Underwood. Pass through Kirkby Underwood village and wood on left. (TF062271) 59ha (145acres)
Forestry Commission

If you are looking for a peaceful place for quiet enjoyment, you'd do well to visit Callans Lane Wood, popular among local residents, particularly at weekends.

A walk along the half-a-mile-long main ride illustrates how work is currently underway to convert the site from conifers, as they reach maturity, to broadleaved woodland.

History enthusiasts might already be aware that the Roman road King Street runs along the boundary. Indeed the ditch and bank system evident at the woodland edges is a pointer to the wood's ancient origin. Other indications are the well-established shrubs and veteran trees that teem with life in the spring. Visit at dawn or at dusk for the chance of spotting deer.

Access is via the long, stony ride which eventually forks into paths that lead around the boundary for the return journey. Tackle these with stout shoes – they can get muddy.

Callans Lane Wood

Twyford Woods
Bourne

Take A151 at Colsterworth, signposted Corby Glen and Bourne. Entrance on right after 800m (0.5 mile). (SK946239) 110ha (272acres)

Forestry Commission

You'll find something of interest year-round at Twyford Woods, even though its proximity to the A1 means it's not the quietest space to relax in.

Great as a 'breath of air' for road travellers, it offers a variety of habitats to explore, from mixed woodland and rough grassland to scrub and wet areas. Well-surfaced tracks and rides provide good access for cyclists and a network of minor paths provide a chance to discover the woodland corners.

Many of the conifers are being removed, prompting a gradual return to broadleaved woodland with strong evidence that ash, birch and willows are regenerating naturally.

The more open areas offer a good display of orchids, while primroses thrive on the ride edges.

Fine orchid display

MAP 4

Morkery Wood
Bourne

From A1 take South Witham
turning, following signs to Castle
Bytham. Car park on right after
2km (1 mile). (SK954192)
157ha (388acres)
Forestry Commission

Morkery Wood is a welcoming
and varied wood — and a great
place to witness the resurgence
of native broadleaved
woodland.

Birch, oak, ash and hazel are
becoming re-established in the
heart of the wood following
the removal of conifers. Stand
atop the ridge for great views
but be aware of continuing
extraction work — and heed
any warning notices.

Besides an asphalt ride from
the car park to the centre of
the wood, all the rides are
hard-surfaced and a series of
paths offer ample opportunities
to explore hidden corners.
Remnants of the original
ancient woodland can be
found on the northeast
boundary which contains
many statuesque boundary
oaks.

The wood's northern edge is
fascinating geologically, with a
number of shake holes and
swallow holes in the limestone,
while a nearby disused quarry
supports a good variety of
wildlife associated with
limestone grassland.

Stapleford Wood

Stapleford Wood
Newark
A17 Coddington roundabout,
signposted Stapleford. (SK874551)
436ha (1078acres)
Forestry Commission

Flat surfaces and a network of
light, well-surfaced rides make
Stapleford Wood a good choice
for easy year-round walking.

While this plantation is
dominated by Scots, Corsican
pine and some pockets of
spruce, a walk to the western
boundary reveals a woodbank
and some veteran oaks. You can
also enjoy pleasant views across
pasture fields from the
woodland edge.

The predominance of
conifers means ground flora is
relatively poor but the verges
of the rides support a much
wider variety of plants such as
white clover, selfheal, sowthistle
and creeping buttercup.

Stapleford Moor, a separate
area of woodland just to the
north, is a quieter and less
mature version of Stapleford
Wood, having been established
from scratch just after the
Second World War.

MAP 4

High Wood
Ancaster

From Sleaford take A17 towards Newark. After 3km (2 miles) turn left towards North Rauceby. At church turn right into Church Lane and wood is on right. Small car park in southern corner of wood. (TF010462) 13ha (32acres)
Woodland Trust

Set atop a gently sloping hill overlooking the old Roman town of Ancaster and providing fine views, the aptly named High Wood is an important landscape feature in an otherwise poorly wooded area.

In spring the heart of the wood is ablaze with violets,

High Wood

which thrive beneath young oak, ash, cherry and willow trees. There are relatively few mature trees in the centre of the wood but the outer edges are fringed with oak, ash and sycamore of a greater age.

A surprising variety of butterflies have been recorded including purple hairstreak, white admiral and white-letter hairstreak – a species usually associated with elm.

Public access is good thanks to a network of paths. But go prepared with suitable footwear when it's wet – some paths can become quite muddy.

Southrey Wood
Bardney or Lincoln
Turn right off B1190 coming from Bardney to Bucknall. (TF129675) 103ha (255 acres)

Forestry Commission

Southrey Wood is full of things to see and learn about, featuring a mixture of tree species that includes oaks, Scots pine and limes.

Great for butterflies, this is a wet woodland served by an extensive series of drainage ditches, which makes aquatic vegetation a feature.

Signs point the way from an open entrance area along a trail of permissive bridleways that take you between an outer layer of blackthorn shrubs and the main heart of the woodland.

The main rides are well maintained and the bridleways make for an interesting trail, though some of the bridges are tricky and wellies are recommended when conditions are wet.

Look out for an area of recently coppiced young limes, two veteran oaks and larger pines which are encountered along the trail.

MAP 4

Tattershall Carrs
Tattershall

From A153 Sleaford to Horncastle road turn north onto B1192 at Conningsby. Wood on left after 800m (0.5 mile). (TF215590) 29ha (71 acres) SSSI

Woodland Trust

Tattershall Carrs forms the last remnant of ancient, wet, alder-dominated woodland that once ringed the margins of the Fens.

It also boasts a fascinating history, for the wood was part of RAF Woodhall Spa during the Second World War – and was home to the famous 617 'Dambusters' squadron. It's still possible to make out bomb shelters and structures within the wood.

Designated a Site of Special Scientific Interest (SSSI) as the most extensive example of ancient alder woodland on the Lincolnshire fens, the site is in fact two woods – Tattershall Thorpe Carr and the larger Tattershall Carr. The alder is particular dominant in the wetter, southern wood, the two being linked by a narrow green lane.

The woods make an attractive destination all year round and contain a wealth of flora and fauna including some nationally scarce insect species and a wide variety of wild flowers. The regionally rare alternate-leaved golden saxifrage is present in the southern wood.

Choose your times to visit as these are wet woods and the paths tend to be muddy in all but the driest of conditions.

Tattershall Carrs

The Pinewoods
Woodhall Spa

Take B1191 towards Horncastle.
Woodhall Spa lies along this road
and wood is on left behind row of
shops. (TF194633) 8ha (19acres)
Woodland Trust

Once part of the landscaped
grounds of the spa, the
woodland is made up of
mature oak, Scots pine, beech
and a lot of regenerating birch.
Decorative trees such as
redwoods and limes have been
introduced in the past.

The Pinewoods are favoured
by lots of wildlife including a
notable range of woodland
birds such as great spotted
woodpeckers, which nest in
mature trees. The importance
of protecting the site was
brought into focus when much
of the surrounding woodland
was lost to development.

It's a great place to enjoy a
walk any time of the year, but
is particularly pleasant during
spring and autumn. There is a
well-used path network,
generally dry under foot.

Ostlers Plantation
Woodhall Spa

Follow B1191 northeast in
Woodhall Spa, then minor road
east towards Kirkby on Bain. Car
park 800m outside Woodhall Spa
on right. (TF215630)
136ha (336acres)
Forestry Commission

Ostlers is a post-war conifer
plantation created on the site
of the famous 'Dambusters'
squadron airfield. Today,
however, the site is one of
tranquillity and beauty.

It's easy to explore, with no
steep climbs and there are
opportunities for youngsters to
play among some interesting
old pines. It's a good place to
take a picnic, with benches
scattered about the plantation.

The wood is almost entirely
Corsican and Scots pine. On
the ground you'll discover an
abundance of bramble
producing their ubiquitous and
delicious crops of soft fruit
in season.

MAP 4

College Wood
Lincoln

At Wragby take B1202 south, at Kingthorpe turn right onto minor road. Wood 1.5km (1 mile) on right. (TF120754) 64ha (158acres)

Forestry Commission

College Wood

Dark and mysterious-looking, College Wood is part of the Bardney Limewoods complex and a wonderful place for children, with a special fairytale quality.

The beauty of the woodland soon emerges as you roam the mix of pines, conifers, spruce, oak, lime, ash and silver birch that makes up a substantial part of the original woodland. One huge veteran oak in particular provides an interesting highlight.

Resident wildlife includes deer, squirrels, pheasant, as well as non-game birds and owls. Look out too for the deer tower.

Access throughout is good, on well-maintained rides but sturdy shoes are recommended.

While there is a good display of woodland flora, particularly in spring, winter can be a good time to enjoy this wood's charms.

Chambers Farm Wood
Lincoln

Take B1202 south from Wragby to Bardney – approx 5km (3 miles). Turn left along Hoop Lane and after 1.5km (1 mile) turn right to wood. (TF149739)

34ha (83acres) SSSI
Forestry Commission

A walk through Chambers Farm Wood provides a feast for

the senses and food for thought.

Set in the heart of the Bardney Limewoods, Chambers gained National Nature Reserve (NNR) status in 1997. It is believed the site has been continuously wooded for thousands of years.

The main rides offer all-weather access for walkers and some for cyclists.

Smaller paths provide ample opportunities to explore and the sharp-eyed can spot not only oak, ash and lime, but also willow, alder, a rich shrub mix and even rarities such as the wild service tree.

The wide rides are managed to encourage butterflies, seen at their best in summer along a specially laid out 'butterfly walk'. Sensitively managed wetland areas support a variety of aquatic fauna and flora.

New Park Wood
Lincoln

A158 from Lincoln to Wragby, take B1202 to Bardney and follow minor road to Waddington. Wood is on sharp right after Lowfield Farm. (TF147705) 166ha (410acres)
Forestry Commission

The area may once have been used for hunting deer and wild boar but little hard evidence remains today.

Most of the woodland – mainly pine and spruce with oak and some small-leaved lime – was planted during the Second World War.

This is a pleasant wood with a well-developed ride system. While there is no waymarking, it is quite open and navigation straightforward. Subsidiary routes can get boggy following rain, so boots are recommended.

Why not combine your visit with a tour of neighbouring Austacre Wood, managed by the Forestry Commission under its Bardney Limewoods conservation plan?

MAP 4

Newball Wood
Lincoln

A158 eastbound from Langworth, pass public house and take right signposted falconry centre. Wood 1.5km (1 mile) on left. (TF082757) 103ha (255acres)
Forestry Commission

Newball Wood

You really feel as though you're discovering an unknown corner of Lincolnshire on a visit to tranquil Newball Wood which, depending on your pace, can take three hours to walk around.

Part of the Bardney Limewood area, the removal of conifers and subsequent regeneration of younger broadleaved trees on this ancient woodland site gives a very open feel. The main species are oak, lime, ash and willow. The reviving ground flora holds the promise of beautiful spring displays.

Bird and bat boxes dot the site – an 'I spy' test for youngsters – and just off the main ride by the entrance is an historical bonus, a moated structure similar to remains in nearby Cucklode Wood.

The main rides are good but can become boggy. You are unlikely to be disturbed by other visitors – but don't jump if you spot a large or exotic raptor – it's probably from the nearby falconry centre!

Hardy Gang Wood
Lincoln

A158 eastbound, take right turn to falconry centre. Follow road for 3km (2 miles) and entrance on right after sharp left turn. (TF090750) 35ha (87acres)

Forestry Commission

This small and ancient wood is currently enjoying a revival.

That's thanks to the Bardney

Limewoods programme, designed to maintain and enhance the special qualities of the area, which is now recognised as a unique and valuable relic of the past.

This site has a good variety with a pretty-even spread of ash, oak, lime and birch. The wood is used for rearing pheasants and closes each Thursday during the shooting season.

Touring the site makes an interesting, 'hardy' walk along some clear and wide main rides though other routes are much narrower and can become difficult in the wet – so wellingtons are a must.

Great West Wood
Lincoln

A158 from Lincoln towards Wragby, take right towards Apley. Wood on right before village. (TF105758) 86ha (213acres)
Forestry Commission

Atmospheric, educational and productive, Great West Wood, near the historic city of Lincoln, is a working woodland with a varied mix of trees.

Separated from its wooded neighbour by a brook, the site is a good place to explore – for those wearing sturdy boots.

At the entrance, four veteran trees stand guard at the gate to the main ride, a wide and seemingly endless route leading right through to Cucklode Wood.

Of the main, well-surfaced ride, are a number of paths that lead through dark tunnels beneath a canopy of pines and small, twisted ash and oak – though some lead nowhere at all.

The wood is populated by a variety of trees with Corsican pine, larch, oak, ash, poplar and some small-leaved lime. Resident wildlife ranges from deer, rabbit and hare to a good variety of bird species.

This is a wet woodland, with drainage ditches throughout the site providing habitats for aquatic vegetation and amphibians.

MAP 4

Old Wood
Lincoln

From Lincoln ring road (A46 bypass) travel west on B1378 to
Skellingthorpe. Wood northwest of Skellingthorpe. (SK905725)
94ha (232acres)
Woodland Trust

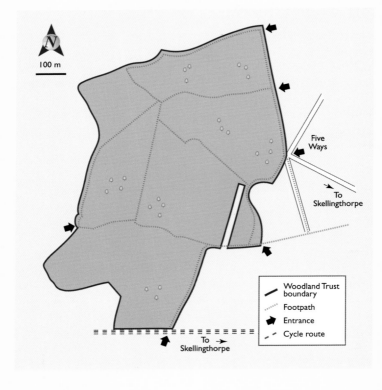

There's a real opportunity to enjoy the 'forest experience' on a visit to expansive Old Wood, an attractive and varied site with a mixture of oak, lime and conifers.

The ancient woodland has a high conservation value which will develop further as the conifer areas, planted during the 1950s and 1960s, are replaced by native species.

The site boasts a wide variety of seasonal flora including twayblade, early-purple orchid, and the beautifully fragrant lily-of-the-valley. Historically the site was important for butterflies but the planting of conifers led to a decline. However a wide variety of wildlife still exists within the wood, owls can often be heard at dusk, and if you are lucky you may glimpse deer at quiet times.

Access is provided by a network of footpaths, cycleway, bridlepaths and public byways from the village of Skellingthorpe, a mile-and-a-half away. Take care when navigating off the path network as it's quite easy to get lost.

Although there are some surfaced paths, other footpaths and bridleways have a tendency to become wet and muddy in the rain, so suitable footwear should be worn.

Old Wood

99

MAP 4

Wickenby Wood
Market Rasen

A46 northeast of Lincoln, take minor road on sharp bend to Friesthorpe. Go through village and at T-junction turn right. Wood on right before level crossing. (TF076824) 46ha (114acres)

Forestry Commission

Wickenby is welcoming and tranquil, with a wide, stoney ride that invites you to discover its variety of broadleaved woodland and ancient remnants, including a historic bank and ditch.

Part of the Bardney Limewoods complex, a group of small-leaved lime lies beyond the hazel-fringed ride.

Dead wood has been retained to encourage mosses, fungi and invertebrates and you may spot bird and bat boxes on your journey. It's worth looking out for deer or listening for nightingale-song emerging from the dense scrub. There is also a variety of wetland habitats including ponds and bog. The soil is clay based and can be muddy – don't forget your boots.

Shooting takes place on this site so please check before you visit.

Wickenby Wood

Willingham Woods
Market Rasen

Take A631 east from Market
Rasen. Car park is 800m (0.5 mile)
past racecourse on left.
(TF137884) 286ha (707acres)
Forestry Commission

Willingham Woods is the
collective name for a group of
fantastically named post-war
plantations including Legsby,
Osgodby, Usselby, Middle
Rasen, Walesby and Dog
Kennel Woods.

These are working woods,
mainly of Scots and Corsican
pine, with regular felling – no
two visits will ever be the same.

Well managed and equipped
for high visitor numbers, the
area is a popular spring and
summer venue for weekend
activities, most centred around
the picnic area and car park.

Visit during quieter times to
enjoy the diverse range of
wildlife that lives in grassland,
wetland and woodland habitats.

Well-surfaced circular paths
provide the chance to go
exploring and some are open
to cyclists. The River Rase
runs through the woods and, in
the centre of the site, are the
remains of a moat.

Willingham Woods

MAP 4

Eleanor Wood & Lynwode Wood

Market Rasen

Off the B1202 4km (2 miles)
south of Market Rasen.
(TF120856) 41ha (101acres)

Forestry Commission

Eleanor and Lynwode woods
are two very different
neighbours linked together by
a narrow strip, offering an
interesting opportunity to
compare and contrast.

Formerly coniferous, Eleanor
Wood is now open, with ash,
oak, and some aspen. Great for
picnics, it has a good ride and
well-managed grassy margins.

Contrast this with Lynwode,
probably derived from Linden
Wood, which still has a strong
presence of lime trees
throughout. Mature conifers
are being removed and the
areas recolonised by birch,
hazel, lime and ash. In the
spring you can find dense
patches of bluebells in the
northeast corner.

You can still see the ancient
woodbank from the edge of
the east–west track, with great
views across to the
countryside beyond.

Owlet Plantation
Gainsborough

From A159 take turning towards
Laughton. In Laughton village turn
left, following signs to Morton.
Wood on left after 4km (2 miles).
(SK825955) 50ha (125acres)

Woodland Trust

For a really rewarding
experience combining open
heath with natural woodland,
Owlet Plantation is well worth
a visit.

Birch, oak and pine areas are
interspersed among more open
heath while scattered
throughout the area you'll find
mature oak trees. Remnant
heath vegetation occurs on
more open areas and is home
to a wealth of butterflies like
the brimstone, small copper
and purple hairstreak, giving
Owlet its Site of Nature
Conservation Interest status.
You might also catch a glimpse
of a nuthatch or a great spotted
woodpecker.

All of this can be enjoyed to
the full by everyone, thanks to
a good circular and surfaced
all-abilities path.

There are a number of
informal paths across the site,
popular with local people, and
those leading to the southern
section are particularly
pleasant. Not far away is a
much larger forested area
known as Laughton Forest and
Laughton Common, which
links to Owlet via a thin strip
of woodland.

WOODLAND
TRUST

Trees and forests are crucial to life on our planet. They generate oxygen, play host to a spectacular variety of wildlife and provide us with raw materials and shelter. They offer us tranquillity, inspire us and refresh our souls.

Founded in 1972, the Woodland Trust is now the UK's leading woodland conservation charity. By acquiring sites and campaigning for woodland it aims to conserve, restore and re-establish native woodland to its former glory. The Trust now owns and cares for over 1,100 woods throughout the UK.

The Woodland Trust wants to see:
no further loss of ancient woodland
the variety of woodland wildlife restored and improved
an increase in new native woodland
an increase in people's understanding and enjoyment of woodland

The Woodland Trust has 150,000 members who share this vision. For every new member, the Trust can care for approximately half an acre of native woodland. For details of how to join the Woodland Trust please either ring FREEPHONE 0800 026 9650 or visit the website at www.woodland-trust.org.uk.

If you have enjoyed the woods in this book please consider leaving a legacy to the Woodland Trust. Legacies of all sizes play an invaluable role in helping the Trust to create new woodland and secure precious ancient woodland threatened by development and destruction. For further information please either call 01476 581129 or visit our dedicated website at www.legacies.org.uk

Major Oak, Sherwood Forest

Further Information

Public transport

Each entry gives a brief description of location, nearest town and grid reference. Traveline provides impartial journey planning information about all public transport services either by ringing 0870 608 2608 (calls charged at national rates) or visit www.traveline.org.uk. For information about the Sustrans National Cycle Network either ring 0117 929 0888 or visit www.sustrans.org.uk

Useful contacts

Forestry Commission, 0845 367 3787, www.forestry.gov.uk
National Trust, 0870 458 4000, www.nationaltrust.org.uk
Wildlife Trusts, 0870 036 7711, www.wildlifetrusts.org
RSPB, 01767 680551, www.rspb.org.uk
Royal Forestry Society, 01442 822028, www.rfs.org.uk
National Community Forest Partnership, 01684 311880, www.communityforest.org.uk
Tree Council, 020 7407 9992, www.treecouncil.org.uk
National Forest, 01283 551211, www.nationalforest.org
Woodland Trust, 01476 581111, www.woodland-trust.org.uk

Recommend a Wood

You can play a part in helping us complete this series. We are inviting readers to nominate a wood or woods they think should be included. We are interested in any woodland with public access in England, Scotland, Wales and Northern Ireland.

To recommend a wood please photocopy this page and provide as much of the following information as possible:

About the wood

Name of wood: _____

Nearest town: _____

Approximate size: _____ ha/acres

Owner/manager: _____

A few words on why you think it should be included:

_____

_____

About you

Your name: _____

Your postal address: _____

_____

_____ Post code: _____

If you are a member of the Woodland Trust please provide your membership number.

Please send to: Exploring Woodland Guides, The Woodland Trust, Autumn Park, Dysart Road, Grantham, Lincolnshire NG31 6LL, by fax on 01476 590808 or e-mail woodlandguides@woodland-trust.org.uk

Thank you for your help

Other Guides in the Series

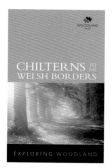

Chilterns to the
Welsh Borders

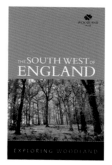

The South West
of England

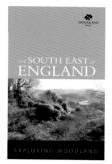

The South East
of England

Wales

Coming soon

East Anglia & North London

Scotland

Yorkshire & the North East

If you would like to be notified when certain titles are due for
publication please either write to Exploring Woodland Guides,
The Woodland Trust, Autumn Park, Dysart Road, Grantham,
Lincolnshire NG31 6LL or e-mail woodlandguides@woodland-
trust.org.uk

Index

Legal & General is delighted to support the Woodland Trust's conservation programme across the UK.

As a leading UK company, Legal & General recognises the importance of maintaining and improving our environment for future generations. We actively demonstrate our commitment through good management and support of environmental initiatives and organisations, such as the Woodland Trust.

Information on how Legal & General manages its impact on the environment can be found at www.legalandgeneralgroup.com/csr.